CARLTON **FOOD** NETWORK

Simply ANTONY

Antony Worrall Thompson

CARLTON FOOD NETWORK From the hit TV series

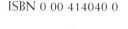

For HarperCollins*Publishers*

Commissioning Editor:
Barbara Dixon
Editor: Becky Humphreys
Proof-readers:
Fiona Screen, Terry Moore

Designer: Clare Baggaley
Photographer: Sian Irvine
Photographer's Assistants:
Jake Curtis and Sara Epstein
Food Stylist: Jane Stevenson
Stylist's Assistant: Lizzy Harris

**Photographs of Antony Worrall
Thompsom**: Mike Lawn

Colour origination and printing by
The Bath Press

CARLTON FOOD NETWORK

Whether you live to eat or eat to live, the Carlton Food Network has something to tempt your tastebuds. Europe's only dedicated food channel brings the expertise of the world's finest chefs, food experts and celebrities to television screens around the country.

Carlton Food Network provides an exciting range of programmes featuring celebrity chefs and personalities such as The Nosh Brothers, Brian Turner, Antony Worrall Thompson, Paul Gayler, Ross Burden, Nanette Newman and many more.

There is something on offer for all food lovers: the great programme line-up features a host of shows presented by the country's top chefs, as well as food from every corner of the world – Africa, India, Italy, China, Scotland, England and Ireland, to mention but a few!

The Carlton Food Network has dedicated itself to ensuring that you know all there is to know about healthy eating and nutrition – so you can really enjoy what you eat. Kids can also try out their culinary skills as the Carlton Food Network features some tasty recipes in a great children's programme – and you can find out how to grow the freshest ingredients to use in the kitchen with the Carlton Food Network's very own gardening slot!

In short, the Carlton Food Network has an exciting mix of ingredients which will appeal to all tastebuds!

Tune into Carlton Food Network, TV's tastiest channel for recipes to make your mouth water.

The author

Antony Worrall Thompson was born in Stratford-upon-Avon, England. Antony studied Hotel and Catering Management at Westminster College, then started his career in cookery as Food and Beverage Manager at a hotel in Essex.

He moved to London in 1978 to become sous chef at Brinkley's Restaurant on the Fulham Road, where he was promoted to head chef in just one month. In 1981, Antony opened Ménage à Trois in Knightsbridge to abundant publicity and reviews: it was the only restaurant to serve just starters and puddings! Since that time, Antony has taken consultancies for a number of companies including, until recently, the Simpson's of Cornhill Group, which includes restaurants such as dell'Ugo, Zoe and Palio. In 1997 Antony opened his latest restaurant, Woz, in Goldbourne Road, North Kensington.

Winner of numerous culinary awards, Antony also finds time to appear regularly on television. He is a 'Ready Steady Cook' regular and a presenter on 'Food and Drink'. He has also filmed three series for Carlton Food Network: 'Simply Antony', 'Quick Cooking with Antony Worrall Thompson' and 'Antony's Taste of Scotland'. Antony's other books include *Supernosh*, with wine writer Malcolm Gluck and *Sainsbury's Quick and Easy Fish*.

NOTES ON THE RECIPES

- *The recipes in this book give ingredients in both metric and imperial, and I suggest you stick to just using one set, in any one recipe.*

- *When a recipe calls for salt and pepper, I recommend you use freshly ground rock salt and black peppercorns.*
- *When a recipe calls for olive oil, use the best quality, extra virgin olive oil that you can afford.*

CONTENTS

INTROD

This book is about really simple cookery. In each chapter I take a well-known food such as chicken, bread or fruit, and take you through a brief introduction to the food, its different varieties, and basic preparation. I then look at really simple cooking methods, so if you've ever wanted to know how to make perfect roast potatoes or even a good boiled egg, I will tell you how. Once I'm sure you feel confident with the basics, I'll go on to tell you how to use these simple techniques in some of my favourite recipes. Some are very straightforward, such as Welsh Rarebit (page 24), others a little trickier, but I take you through them step-by-step, so success is guaranteed.

The secrets of successful cooking:

1 Get the basics right first. A well-made cheese omelette is much more satisfying to eat than a complicated dish, that has caused you heart-ache to produce. Lots of people claim that they never enjoy meals they have cooked themselves, and this is often because they have slaved over a hot stove, and have worried themselves half to death. It is so much better to prepare something simple, and to spend time enjoying it (and enjoying your guests, if entertaining), than fussing in the kitchen. Once you have mastered a few basic dishes, by all means, move onto something a little more time consuming and complex. But I suggest

UCTION

you don't try anything new when you have guests over. Sod's Law dictates that it is bound to go horribly wrong (possibly induced by a glass of wine or two during preparation!).

2 Buy the best quality ingredients you can. Using fresh, good quality ingredients will ensure a good flavour. A simple salad, using the freshest ingredients, for example, is very easy, and absolutely delicious. Quite simply, if you can't find or afford the best quality ingredients that the recipe calls for, try another recipe for now. For example. I list jumbo prawns in the ingredients list for Stir-fry cellophane noodle with prawns. Using small prawns would result

in a rather insubstantial dish, and would waste the money spent on the other ingredients.

3 Have a go! We all had to start somewhere, and it is through trial and error that we learn. Once you feel confident with a couple of basic recipes under your belt, and you are getting familiar with the food group, then I'm sure you won't go too far wrong. And even if it doesn't quite look like you imagined, chances are it will still taste pretty good!

Antony Worrall Thompson

The
Kitchen equipment

Let's start with the absolute basics. I assume you have a kitchen at this point, so let's look at the kitchen equipment you will need. I hope this doesn't look like a daunting list – many of these pieces of equipment are inexpensive, and the more expensive items should last you a good while (a lifetime in many cases), so they are worth the investment. They will help to make your cooking easier, which is what this book is all about. Remember, these are just the basics – there are hundreds of kitchen gadgets you can buy, and the number is ever-increasing as culinary fashions come and go, but most of them aren't essential.

If you are going to spend some money in your kitchen, spend it on good knives, a sharpening steel and a couple of good pans. They can last a lifetime, and are worth it.

PARING KNIFE *A small knife with a slightly curved blade. Designed for peeling, it is also useful for slicing small items.*

FLEXIBLE BLADE KNIFE *A small knife, good for cutting fish.*

15 CM/6 IN COMMON OR GARDEN KNIFE *Firm, sharp, and good for all sorts of things.*

LARGE BLADE SASHIMI *Good for carving meat.*

BUTCHER'S KNIFE *Strong, heavy blade designed for jointing meat, but useful for all sorts of tasks.*

SHARPENING STEEL *Essential for sharpening your knives; a blunt knife is dangerous because it is likely to slip.*

HEAVY-BOTTOMED PANS *Buy a large, medium and small pan, each with lids.*

NON-STICK FRYING PANS *Space-age Teflon is fantastic stuff – a real boon in the kitchen. You'll need two or three non-stick frying pans. A large pan can double-up as a wok.*

BASICS

MIXING BOWLS *You will need one large bowl, and one or two smaller ones. Stainless steel is the cheapest, and fine for the job in hand.*

BAKING TRAYS AND DISHES *You could buy these as and when a recipe calls for them, or you might find a good-value set. You are going to need flan tins, muffin tins, loaf tins, a roasting dish and baking sheet.*

GRIDDLE PAN *This allows you to achieve a healthy, attractive grilled effect using a hob.*

TRIVET *This is a stable, wooden base, essential for protecting kitchen surfaces from hot pans.*

KITCHEN PAPERS *You'll need a constant supply of clingfilm, foil and greaseproof paper.*

JUICER *You can buy electric ones, if you plan to drink lots of fruit and vegetable juice, but a small hand juicer will do for the odd lemon or lime.*

PESTLE AND MORTAR *A small, marble one is ideal, and fairly inexpensive.*

ROLLING PIN *Essential now that milk bottles are hard to come by.*

MEASURING SPOONS *Buy a set of measuring spoons, as a cook's teaspoon is not the same as the one we use to stir tea.*

WHISK *A small hand whisk and a larger balloon whisk will be fine.*

COLANDER *For draining vegetables and pasta.*

FOOD PROCESSOR/BLENDER *Expensive, but extremely useful gadgets to have in the kitchen.*

You'll also need a measuring jug, a sieve, a few wooden spoons and assorted forks, mashers and draining spoons.

Stocks

I'm not a pedant about this; use a stock cube if you want to. Life is short, and I am a realist, but one word of advice – use the best stock cubes you can afford; some of them really are excellent, but if cooking becomes a hobby, you might like to make your own stock. You can make a whole range of stocks – chicken, vegetable, beef, fish, veal, game... basically, whatever you fancy, but I am going to tell you how to make the three staples – chicken, vegetable and fish. They are invaluable for giving flavour and substance to soups, casseroles and sauces.

CHICKEN STOCK

Makes about 2.75 litres/5 pints

This is a very simple stock to make, and is the one that I use most. This recipe makes a white (or 'blonde') chicken stock. If you use bones which have been roasted, you will get a brown stock. You can freeze stock, but if you want to make a smaller quantity, reduce the ingredients proportionately.

2 tablespoons olive oil
1.75 kg/4 lb chicken bones
2 carrots, chopped
1 celery stick, chopped
1 leek, sliced
1 onion, quartered
1 glass of dry white wine
1 bay leaf
grated rind of 1 lemon
small bunch of thyme
6 peppercorns

1 Heat the oil in a very large, cast iron pan then cook the chicken bones and vegetables for about 3 minutes.
2 Pour the wine over the chicken bones and vegetables and add enough water to cover.
3 Add the bay leaf, lemon rind, thyme and peppercorns and bring to the boil. Cover, and simmer gently for 4 hours. There should be hardly any movement else the stock will go cloudy. During the cooking, remove any scummy bits that rise to the surface of the stock using a metal spoon.
4 Pour the stock through a colander into a clean pan, and discard the vegetables and bones. Bring the stock to a fast boil, then leave to cool. Freeze in small containers, ready for use.

Sauces

VEGETABLE STOCK

Basically, you can use whichever vegetables you like to make vegetable stock. Onions and carrots are pretty much essential, and tomatoes add welcome flavour, so add a few of them, but beyond that, use whatever you fancy. Simply chuck a load of chopped vegetables into a cast iron pan and cover with water. Bring to the boil, cover, and simmer for 4 hours. Sieve to remove any large chunks that still remain. Vegetable stock is quite bland in itself, but is a very useful base for lighter soups and sauces.

FISH STOCK

Fish stock is the only stock that doesn't take hours to cook, so it's worth having a go at this one. Finely chop a selection of vegetables (leeks, shallots, celery and carrots are good) and place in a cast iron pan with some fish bones. Cover with water, bring to the boil and simmer gently for just 20 minutes. Sieve, and freeze your fish stock ready for use.

NOTE

To make beef or veal stock takes at least 8 hours cooking time, and is particularly messy, so is therefore best left to someone else!

BÉCHAMEL (WHITE) SAUCE
makes 600 ml/1 pint

Béchamel is not so in fashion at the moment, which is a real shame, because it is very useful, and, when made properly, delicious. For extra flavour, 'infuse' the milk by boiling it with an onion, clove and bay leaf, for a minute or two. You could also add double cream for extra richness (not single cream, as it will separate in the sauce).

50 g/2 oz butter
50 g/2 oz flour
600 ml/1 pint milk
pinch of salt
freshly ground black or white pepper
pinch of nutmeg (optional)

1 Melt the butter over a low heat in a saucepan.
2 Add the flour and stir briskly until the mixture is smoothly blended, but don't let it change colour. This mixture is called a 'roux'.

3 Add the milk, a little at a time, and stir well with a wooden spoon to prevent any lumps forming. If any lumps do appear, simply stir more vigorously until they disappear. As a last resort, you can sieve it.
4 Season with salt and pepper and, if you wish, a pinch of nutmeg. Continue to cook for about 10 minutes, stirring occasionally to prevent a skin forming.

VARIATIONS

You can use béchamel sauce as a base for a wide range of sauces. Try adding onions, mushrooms, white wine, cheese, tomato purée, tarragon, parsley or chopped egg.

HOLLANDAISE SAUCE
Makes about 450 ml/¾ pint

The classic hollandaise sauce uses cubes of cold butter, but this recipe works just as well using melted butter. There are many variations based on this classic sauce: add 1 tablespoon orange juice to make Maltaise sauce; 4 tablespoons whipped cream to make Mousseline sauce; diced tomato and tomato purée for Sharon sauce, and fried, chopped shallots, white wine, tarragon, red wine vinegar and cayenne pepper for béarnaise sauce.

500 g/1 lb butter
5 medium egg yolks
1 tablespoon lemon juice
freshly ground black pepper

1 Pour 3 tablespoons of water into a small saucepan with a pinch of freshly ground black pepper. Place the base of the pan in a *bain-marie* or large saucepan containing tepid water.
2 In another saucepan, melt the butter without letting it get too hot.
3 Beat the egg yolks with 1 tablespoon of water and pour into the pan containing the warmed water. With the pan still in the *bain-marie*, whisk the sauce until the yolks thicken to the consistency of thick cream.
4 Slowly add the melted butter and 2 tablespoons of water, whisking all the time. Adjust the seasoning to taste, and add the lemon juice. Whisk again, and then remove from the *bain-marie* or saucepan until ready to serve.

MAYONNAISE
Makes about 300 ml/½ pint

1 large egg yolk
1 tablespoon Dijon mustard
150 ml/¼ pint olive oil
150 ml/¼ pint vegetable oil
juice of 1 lemon
salt and freshly ground black pepper

1 Beat the egg yolk vigorously, for 1 minute, in a *bain-marie* or in a small bowl over a small saucepan full of simmering water.
2 Remove from the pan and add both oils, drop by drop at first, then in a thin, steady stream, whisking continuously for about 4 minutes, or until the mayonnaise is thick.
3 Add the lemon juice and season with salt and freshly ground black pepper to taste.

NOTE

If your mayonnaise starts to curdle, mix 1 tablespoon cold water or lemon juice, and slowly work it into the mayonnaise.

Reductions

In the trendy 80s, reductions were all the rage. No one used the old classic sauces such as béchamel. Reductions are one of the few elements of nouvelle cuisine that have survived, and quite rightly so, because they are very easy to make – and very delicious.

A reduction, simply, is a concentrated sauce or stock, which you make by boiling your liquid until it reduces in volume. How long you boil it for depends on the quantity of liquid and the degree of concentration required. The object of reducing a sauce is to improve its flavour, smoothness and consistency.

You would serve reductions with any piece of meat, and it is worth reducing the cooking juices from a piece of meat to give a very tasty gravy.

Try this simple recipe for a reduction sauce: mix together 3 tablespoons of white wine vinegar, 2 tablespoons of water, and a few crushed peppercorns. Heat in a pan until the liquid reduces to about 1 tablespoon. Use this as a basic sauce, or try:

❧ adding ½ glass of wine, a pinch of saffron and a dollop of butter. Cook until the butter has melted, then bring back to the boil. Finally, add 2 tablespoons of double cream for a really fattening sauce that will go straight to your hips. You will only need to serve a dribble of this, as it is very rich.

❧ adding a large dollop of butter and some chopped, fresh herbs. Stir until the butter has melted, then boil to reduce. Season with freshly ground black pepper, for a simple, but fattening herb sauce.

DAIRY

Cream

I thought I'd start with the most 'sinful' of the lot. I guess it's got some vitamins in it, but the main reason for using cream is that it tastes great.

The cream to use for sauces is double cream, with its high fat content (48% fat). Single cream (18% fat) is good for pouring, but it splits if used for cooking. The extra thick double cream that you can buy is artificially thickened; I'm not convinced it's worth paying extra for. Clotted cream is wonderful for dolloping on things. Soured cream is very useful for fish dishes and baking. If you have any left over, dollop it on top of a large baked potato. Crème fraîche is a French cream product, which makes a good accompaniment to puddings – whenever we'd use double cream really. The French also use it for cooking. Ironically, as we start to buy more and more crème fraîche, the French are buying our double cream. *C'est la vie!*

And then there are the 'almost-creams'. Mascarpone and fromage frais are used like creams, but are actually soft cheeses. Their texture and flavour make them ideal to serve with fruit and desserts. If you are terrified of piling on the pounds, my hint to you is use more yoghurt. Greek yoghurt, especially, is great for cooking; you can use it in all the same recipes as double cream, but it has about $\frac{1}{5}$th of the fat content. It is also ideal for adding thickness and a slightly sour taste to curries. Simply stir it into curries at the end of the cooking time, as you would with double cream.

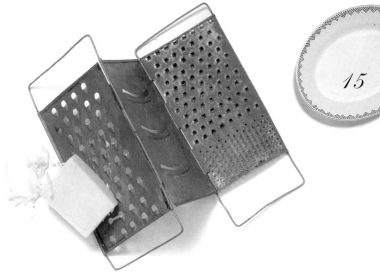

HOW TO MAKE PROPER CUSTARD
Makes about 600 ml/1 pint

1 vanilla pod
2 tablespoons double cream
500 ml/18 fl oz milk
5 egg yolks
125 g/4 oz sugar

1 Split and scrape the vanilla pod, and place the pod and seeds into the double cream and milk. Bring to the boil gently, and then simmer for 2-3 minutes.

2 Meanwhile, whisk together the egg yolks and sugar in a separate bowl until pale.

3 Remove the vanilla pod from the milk and slowly whisk the warm milk and cream mixture into the eggs.

4 Pour the mixture into a clean saucepan and heat gently until the custard starts to thicken. You could cook this over a *bain-marie* if you like. Be careful not to boil the custard, else the eggs will start to scramble. Cook for about 6 minutes. The mixture should still be runny. If the custard gets too thick, plunge the saucepan into a bowl of iced water to arrest the cooking.

NOTE
If you are fed-up trying to keep a bowl steady while you whisk something, rest the bowl on a cloth to keep it stable.

CRÈME BRÛLÉE
Serves 6

This is also known as burnt custard or Cambridge burnt custard. The origins of this dessert are unclear; both the French and a Cambridge college claim to have invented it!

Make the custard (as described left), and pour into ramekin dishes. There should be enough to fill 6 individual ramekins. Place in a fridge to set overnight. Just before serving, cover the tops of the custards with caster sugar, and then grill the top until the sugar turns dark brown and caramelised. Most domestic grills aren't hot enough, so if you place the ramekins in a baking tray containing iced water, this will help to prevent the custard from separating while you wait for the sugar to melt. Alternatively, invest in a small blow torch.

Chocolate ICE CREAM

You need an ice cream machine to make this. You could make it by hand, but it takes forever.

serves 4

1 vanilla pod
450 ml/¾ pint double cream
300 ml/½ pint milk
5 egg yolks
125 g/4 oz caster sugar
100 g/3½ oz plain chocolate

1 Split and scrape the vanilla pod, and place the pod and seeds into 150 ml/¼ pint of the double cream and milk. Bring to the boil gently, and then simmer for 2-3 minutes.

2 Meanwhile, whisk together the egg yolks and sugar in a separate bowl until pale.

3 Remove the vanilla pod from the milk and slowly whisk the warm milk and cream mixture into the eggs.

4 Pour the mixture into a clean pan and heat gently until the custard starts to thicken. You could cook this over a *bain-marie* if you like. Be careful not to boil the custard, else the eggs will start to scramble. Cook for about 6 minutes. You should be able to coat the back of a wooden spoon. Strain the custard into a cold bowl.

5 Melt the chocolate in a *bain-marie* and then stir into the custard.

6 Whisk the remaining double cream and add to the chocolate custard. Pour the ice-cream mix into an ice-cream machine and allow it to churn and chill until the ice-cream is fairly solid. Serve at once or chill in the freezer until ready to serve.

Opposite
Back: Tortilla (page 21), *front:* Mozzarella in Carozza (page 26).

Overleaf
Back: Tabbouleh (page 36), *front:* Stir-fry Cellophane Noodles with Prawns (page 32).

Balsamic strawberries with MASCARPONE CREAM

Balsamic vinegar brings out the wonderful flavour of strawberries in a way not possible with sugar alone.

serves 4-6

1 kg/2 lb ripe strawberries, stalks and hulls removed

4 tablespoons balsamic vinegar

6 tablespoons caster sugar

3 egg yolks

4 teaspoons Kirsch

250 g/8 oz mascarpone cheese

150 ml/¼ pint double cream

1 Soak the strawberries in the balsamic vinegar with 4 tablespoons of caster sugar for at least half an hour, stirring from time to time.

2 Meanwhile, beat the remaining caster sugar with the egg yolks until very pale. Fold in the Kirsch and the mascarpone cheese.

3 Whisk the cream into soft peaks and fold into the mascarpone mixture. Serve with the strawberries.

TZATZIKI

This is great served with toasted pitta bread, as a starter or a dip.

serves 4

1 cucumber, grated

1 small tub Greek yoghurt

salt and freshly ground black pepper

1 teaspoon roasted cumin seeds

1 Blot the grated cucumber using kitchen paper, to remove some moisture.

2 Mix the cucumber with the Greek yoghurt, salt, pepper and the cumin seeds.

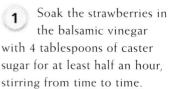
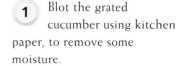

Eggs

There are almost as many varieties of egg available today as there are egg controversies. Duck, hen, goose, quail, free-range, corn-fed... there is plenty of choice, but let's keep it simple by saying buy free-range – for two very good reasons:

❦ the hens are better treated

❦ they are more likely to be salmonella-free

Sure, they cost a bit more, but the price difference is negligible in a weekly shop, and the only way the price will come down is if we all try to buy free-range eggs, and if the government sorts out egg farming.

Quails eggs are very dinky, but totally ridiculous unless you are really trying to impress an egg fanatic.

Some eggs now come with a use-by date stamped on the side – but if you buy some old-fashioned eggs, and have forgotten how long they have been sitting in the fridge, the easy way to tell if they are still fresh is to place them in a bowl of tepid water. If they float they are past their best.

STORING EGGS

Eggs will keep for a couple of days if kept at room temperature; you only need to put them in a fridge if keeping them for a week. Many recipes work best if you use eggs at room temperature. Bear in mind that eggs absorb nearby flavours, so keep them in a sealed container.

HOW TO BOIL AN EGG

This may seem very simple to you, but there are some people to whom this will seem like a culinary challenge; my grandmother, for one, would burn an egg. The trick is to start with a pan of cold water. If you put a cold egg into boiling water, the shell will crack, and bits of egg will leak out. Lower your egg into the water on a spoon. If you just plonk your egg into the pan, it will probably hit the bottom of the pan and bounce up again, cracked. Bring the water to the boil. Boil for 3 minutes for a runny egg, 6 minutes for a soft/medium egg (chefs call this 'mollet', and it's the perfect consistency for serving eggs in salads) and 9 minutes for a hard-boiled egg. Whether you crack or cut the top of the egg is up to you, but you must serve it with hot, buttered toast soldiers.

HOW TO POACH AN EGG

Start with a large pan of boiling water. Add a good
slug of malt or red wine vinegar to the water, but no
salt (this will cause the egg to break up). Break your
egg into a small cup, then slide the egg into the
water. Boil the egg for 2 minutes, and then
scoop it out. You can serve it immediately, or
plunge it into ice cold water, which will arrest
the cooking time. This is useful for salads. You
could do this the night before, and simply
reheat by throwing into a pan of boiling water
for a couple of seconds – but this is only necessary
if you really aren't a morning person.

HOW TO FRY AN EGG

Most people fry eggs in oil – I think you get the
best flavour from frying in butter. Use a good, non-
stick frying pan, and add a generous knob of butter.
Melt the butter over a gentle heat, and carefully
break the egg into the pan. Baste the egg with the
melted butter continuously, until the yolk goes
cloudy. It will only take 2-3 minutes. When your
egg is ready, carefully remove it from the pan using
a fish slice. Serve seasoned with salt and pepper on
unbuttered toast – you really don't need any more
butter at this stage! Some people like to fry their
eggs using small, circular moulds, which is neater,
but it isn't really necessary.

HOW TO SCRAMBLE EGGS

There are two ways to do this – the English way, and the French way:

ENGLISH

Have your toast ready. Melt a large knob of butter in a pan. Lightly beat 3 eggs with a fork, and pour them into the pan. Using a wooden spoon, lightly stir the eggs for 1-2 minutes, and then tip onto your toast. They will look very soft, but be assured they will continue to cook when removed from the pan. Season with a little salt and pepper. You could serve this with a few slices of smoked salmon for a special breakfast or brunch, or you could stir in a teaspoon of horseradish while cooking the eggs.

FRENCH

Start by whisking your eggs, hard. Melt a knob of butter in a pan, and pour in the eggs. Whisk for 2 minutes and add 4 tablespoons of double cream, gradually, during the cooking time. Season with salt and pepper and serve. You get much finer, richer scrambled eggs this way, which are wonderful (though extremely fattening) served on their own.

BUTTER-CRUMBED EGGS

Kids love this crunchy egg dish, but it is also very good for adults, served on a bed of salad as a starter, or for brunch or breakfast. Poach an egg as described on page 19. When ready, lift the egg out and dry on some kitchen paper. Trim the egg a little, to tidy the edges, and then coat in some whisked egg yolk. Roll the egg in a plate of breadcrumbs, then fry the coated eggs in some melted butter, for about 2 minutes on each side.

WHISKING EGG WHITES

Before whisking egg whites, wipe the bowl with lemon juice. This is a sure-fire way of getting your egg whites to whisk up, as it removes any last, invisible traces of grease.

TORTILLA (Spanish omelette)

The Spanish wouldn't use thyme in this dish, but I love the flavour, so why not try it both ways? You can serve this hot or cold, or cut in slices. You could add cooked ham, chicken or smoked fish to the basic mixture at step 3. (*Shown opposite page 16*)

serves 6

2 tablespoons olive oil for shallow frying

750 g/1½ lb potatoes, peeled and cut into slices

2 red onions, sliced

6 eggs, beaten

3 roasted red peppers, peeled and cut into quarters

500 g/1 lb spinach, drained, chopped and squeezed and mixed with 1 tablespoon olive oil

small bunch thyme, chopped

salt and freshly ground black pepper

1 Heat 1 tablespoon of oil in a large frying pan, add some salt and pepper and shallow-fry the potatoes for 4-5 minutes. Drain off some of the oil, leaving just a little showing in the pan.

2 Add the onions to the potatoes and fry for 2 minutes until just soft. Drain the mixture through a colander and discard the oil.

3 Beat the eggs in a separate bowl, and season with salt and pepper. Add the potato and onion mixture, the roast peppers, spinach and thyme, and stir.

4 Heat the remaining oil in the pan and add the egg mixture. Cook for 10 minutes, without stirring. The tortilla should be solid at the base – it shouldn't wobble if you shake it. Take the pan and place it under a grill for a minute or two or until the top turns golden brown.

5 Remove the pan from the grill, and blot the top of the tortilla with kitchen towel to remove any excess oil. Place a plate on the top of the tortilla and turn the pan over to tip the tortilla out. Serve hot or cold, cut into thick slices.

Cheese

There are thousands of cheeses around the world, and there are more appearing all the time. We have hard cheeses, cream cheeses, soft cheeses, and ones with all sorts of flavours and strengths. Only a few years ago, most of us had never heard of mozzarella, ricotta and halloumi, and now they are commonplace. The French have always lead the way in cheeses, prompting President de Gaulle to ask "How can I rule a nation with over 400 cheeses?"

Parmesan has come a long way from the little tubs of tasteless powder we once used to sprinkle on our spaghetti bolognese. Several fresh varieties are now available in all the supermarkets and it's worth keeping a block in your fridge. It adds lots of flavour to lots of recipes, and I suggest you try it on its own – delicious eaten with a pear.

Stilton is an underused cheese – too often associated with old men and port, but I think it's due for a revival.

You need to be selective with the Cheddar you buy. There are rows upon rows of cheap, mild Cheddar on sale in the supermarkets, because shoppers seem to want a cheese that the whole family can eat i.e. mild. I personally like something with a little more character.

Emmenthal is often served on a cheeseboard, and I think it is excellent for cooking, but not so good for eating on its own. Choose something else.

Baked garlic & goat's CHEESE custards

This is delicious served with just a few salad leaves, or if you are feeling in the mood for something a bit tangier, add a garnish of capers, roast peppers, anchovies and black olives mixed in olive oil.

serves 2

12 cloves garlic, blanched in boiling water for 5 minutes

300 ml/½ pint milk

2 sprigs thyme

1 bay leaf

100 g/3½ oz soft fresh goat's cheese

1 egg

2 egg yolks

150 ml/¼ pint double cream

salt and freshly ground black pepper

1 Simmer the blanched garlic in the milk with the thyme and bay leaf, until it is quite soft.

2 Discard the thyme and bay leaf and pour the milk into a food processor with the garlic and goat's cheese. Whizz until puréed.

3 Beat the egg and egg yolks well, and stir into the double cream. Add to the mixture in the food processor and whizz until combined.

4 Pour the prepared mixture into two buttered 150 ml/¼ pint soufflé dishes and place on a baking tray lined with a tea towel. Pour in hot water to cover the tea towel and to come halfway up the sides of the soufflé dishes. Bake for 25 minutes in a preheated oven at gas mark 3/160°C/325°F until set. Serve while still warm.

Welsh RAREBIT

This Welsh Rarebit mixture can be made up and kept in a fridge. Cheddar cheese is the traditional cheese for this recipe, but you could also try it with a crumbly cheese such as Cheshire. Serve this recipe on its own, or topped with crispy bacon or a poached egg.

250 g/8 oz Cheddar, grated
1 teaspoon English mustard
2 teaspoons beer
1 tablespoon Worcester sauce
25 g/1 oz softened butter
2 slices thick, white bread

serves 1

1 Whizz the cheese, mustard, beer, Worcester sauce and butter together in a food processor, until smooth.

2 Toast the bread on one side only. Spread the cheese paste on the untoasted side and grill the slices for about 3 minutes or until the cheese bubbles. Serve immediately.

CHEESE Sauce

This is useful either served with fish or a vegetable dish, or as a base for soufflé. Gruyère or Emmenthal is ideal for a cheese sauce; I find Cheddar too greasy. A little grated Parmesan adds a good flavour, if you have some handy.

makes about 600 ml/1 pint

600 ml/1 pint milk
1 onion
1 bay leaf
1 clove
50 g/2 oz butter
50 g/2 oz flour
75 g/3 oz Gruyère, grated
salt and freshly ground
black pepper

1 Heat the milk in a large, heavy-based pan together with the onion, bay leaf and clove, and leave to simmer for 20 minutes.

2 Meanwhile, in a clean pan, melt the butter and then gradually stir in the flour. Cook for 2 minutes over a low heat, stirring constantly.

3 Remove the onion, bay leaf and clove, and gradually start to add the milk to the flour and butter. Keep the pan at a low heat. You will need to add the milk very slowly, stirring all the time. This will take about 5 minutes.

4 Once all the milk has been added and the sauce has started to thicken, add the cheese and stir in until melted. Season with salt and freshly ground black pepper.

MOZZARELLA in Carozza

This is basically a fried mozzarella sandwich. You can add anything you like, and I suggest you try it with roasted red peppers, Parma ham or a bit of grated Parmesan. (*Shown opposite page 16*)

serves 1

3 tablespoons olive oil

1 shallot, peeled and finely sliced

2 slices bread (thick, sliced white or a fancy Italian bread – it's up to you), crusts removed

milk for coating

50 g/2 oz buffalo mozzarella, thinly sliced

1 sun-dried tomato, sliced

flour, lightly seasoned, to coat

1 egg, beaten

breadcrumbs, for coating

1 Heat 1 tablespoon of oil in a medium-sized frying pan, and gently fry the shallot for 2-3 minutes. Meanwhile, brush one side of each slice of bread with milk.

2 Place the slices of mozzarella on the brushed side of the bread, and then top with the cooked shallot and the sun-dried tomato. Cover with the other slice of bread, milk side down, and press down the edges to seal the sandwich.

3 Dip the sandwich in the seasoned flour, then the beaten egg, and then in a plate of breadcrumbs, until well coated. Be sure to let the egg soak well into the bread.

4 Heat the rest of the oil in a pan and then shallow fry the sandwich for 3 minutes on each side, or until crispy and brown. The oil will need to be deep enough to come half way up the sides of the sandwiches, to ensure it is cooked all the way round.

CHEESE soufflé

If you want a really high soufflé, you will need to add a paper collar inside the soufflé dish, but I find that high soufflés are dry. I like a soufflé to be slightly soft and floppy.

serves 4

25 g/1 oz butter, plus extra for greasing

3 tablespoons freshly grated Parmesan

2 tablespoons plain flour

1 cup warm milk

3 tablespoons freshly grated Gruyère

4 egg yolks, beaten for 1 minute until paler in colour

5 egg whites

salt and freshly ground black pepper

1 Butter a 1 litre/1¾ pint soufflé dish (or 4 small ramekins), then tip in 1 tablespoon of the Parmesan and coat the sides and base.

2 Melt 25 g/1 oz butter in a small saucepan. Stir in the flour and cook over a moderate heat, stirring for 2 minutes. Gradually add the milk, stirring continuously. Bring to the boil and then reduce the heat to simmer the sauce for 5 minutes.

3 Stir in the Gruyère and remaining Parmesan and then the egg yolks, one at a time. Season to taste. Transfer the mixture to a large mixing bowl.

4 Whisk the egg whites until they form soft peaks (not firm) and then tip half on top of the cheese sauce. Using a metal spoon, lift and fold the egg whites into the mixture. Repeat with the remaining egg whites.

5 Spoon the mixture gently (not from a great height) into the prepared dish (or into 4 individual dishes) and run your thumb or a teaspoon around the edge of the soufflé. It will rise within this flattened edge. If you like, sprinkle a little more grated Parmesan on top. Bake the soufflé in a preheated oven at gas mark 6/200°C/400°F for 10 minutes. Do not open the oven door during this time! When the soufflé is well risen and pale brown, open the door very slowly and remove the soufflé. Serve immediately.

PASTA &

Pasta & noodles

Once upon a time there was spaghetti and, in really sophisticated households, lasagne. Now we have a myriad of different types of pasta, and they are the new mainstay of our diets, offering countless new eating ideas. We have pasta of all colours and shapes and sizes, made with all sorts of ingredients, and from all over the globe. We have (of course) a huge variety of pasta from Italy and its communities around the world, but don't forget all the pasta that comes from the Orient, such as vermicelli and Chinese noodles. And there's pasta you can stuff or bake or cover in sauce... the varieties are never ending. You can also buy pasta stuffed with all manner of delicious things – we are no longer just confined to dodgy tinned ravioli – there are delicious varieties available in all supermarkets, including goat's cheese and ricotta.

There's a debate about which is better – dried or fresh pasta, and I can honestly say that I think dried pasta is better for most recipes. Fresh pasta, although all the rage at the moment, is made with a type of flour that seems to make it go soggy. Dried uses a hard wheat, which, when cooked properly, gives that lovely 'bite' we talk about when cooking pasta.

Pasta is really easy to cook. Boil a large

GRAINS

pan of water, and add a little salt. Don't use oil, as some people may recommend. Add your pasta, and give it a quick stir to stop it sticking together. Bring back to the boil and let the water simmer. Make sure you read the instructions on the packet, because some pastas need soaking rather than cooking (some noodles, for example), and they all take slightly different times to cook, depending on thickness. A basic rule is that fresh pasta will take just 2-3 minutes to cook, whereas dried pasta takes 8-12 minutes. My wife suggests that you throw a piece of the pasta at a wall to test if it is cooked – if it sticks, it is ready to eat. Drain the pasta – and it's ready to use.

QUICK TOMATO SAUCE

This is perfect for making in a big batch and keeping in the fridge or freezer. Use whatever quantities you have to hand – it's such a staple that it is worth experimenting with amounts to see what suits you.

Heat some good olive oil in a large, heavy-based pan. Gently fry some chopped onions, garlic and add some dried or fresh oregano. Add a couple of tins of plum tomatoes (chopped, or whole, with juice). You could use fresh tomatoes, but I often find that the tomatoes found in supermarkets have virtually no flavour, so it's not worth the extra expense. I'd suggest you add some passata (sieved and bottled tomato) too, which will add a lovely rich flavour. Cook for 10-15 minutes and season with freshly ground black pepper. You could stir in some grated Parmesan, and a small handful of torn basil leaves too.

TIP

Don't smother your pasta with sauce – that's a very British trait, and it's unnecessary.

How to make
GNOCCHI

A simple
GNO

This is so cheap and easy to make, please don't be tempted to buy ready-made gnocchi.

serves 4

500 g/1 lb mashed potatoes (ordinary, floury potatoes or sweet potatoes, or even semolina)
2 egg yolks
2 tablespoons flour

1. Beat all the ingredients together with a wooden spoon, or use your hands. Beat or knead thoroughly.

2. Take a small piece of the potato dough, and roll into a ball about the size of a ping-pong ball. Flatten slightly with a fork. This is your first gnocchi, and you need to do this to the rest of the dough. When you have made all the gnocchi, refrigerate for a couple of hours.

3. When you are ready to cook them, remove from the fridge, and cook in boiling salted water. They are cooked when they float.

I have said use either Gorgonzola or Dolcelatta for this recipe, but they are basically the same cheese. The Italians call it Gorgonzola, and the Brits call it Dolcelatta – I can only assume we have a different taste in names.

serves 4

25 g/1 oz butter
6 shallots, chopped
½ glass dry vermouth
250 ml/8 fl oz double cream
a large handful of spinach
125 g/4 oz Gorgonzola or Dolcelatta, crumbled
50 g/2 oz Parmesan, grated
1 quantity of gnocchi (see left)
50 g/2 oz breadcrumbs
salt and freshly ground black pepper

Paneer - Capture a Taste of India

Paneer is a truly authentic Indian ingredient originating from the Punjab region. 100% vegetarian, Paneer is a natural meat substitute, which is commonly included in Asian cookery. Whether cubed, sliced, grated or crumbled, Paneer takes on the flavours that it is cooked with. Paneer has a life of many weeks and can be easily frozen, making it a versatile cooking ingredient.

Paneer is currently available in selected Tesco, Sainsbury's, Somerfield, Waitrose and Asda stores.

Paneer Jalfrezi

Ingredients

227g / ½lb Paneer
½ green pepper
½ red pepper
1 small onion
1 small courgette
2 carrots
3 mushrooms
50g / 2oz beansprouts
½ teaspoon salt
1 teaspoon sugar
the juice of ½ a lemon
113g / ¼lb of tinned tomatoes
½ teaspoon cumin seeds
1 teaspoon oil

Method

Chop all of the vegetables and cut the Paneer into strips (julienne style).

Heat the oil in a wok or large pan. Add the cumin seeds for a few seconds, then add the tomatoes and carrots. Heat for a further two minutes, stirring all the time.

Add the rest of the vegetables and heat until they are almost cooked, stirring all the time.

Finally, add the Paneer and cook for a further few minutes. Mix well and serve immediately.

Serves 2 - 3

Tandoori Paneer

Ingredients

227g / ½lb Paneer cut into small cubes
¼ teaspoon chilli powder
¼ teaspoon freshly ground black pepper
small piece of fresh ginger, ground to a paste
1 garlic clove, crushed
½ teaspoon paprika
¼ pint plain unsweetened yoghurt
few drops lemon juice
oil
orange food colouring (optional)

Method

Mix together the chilli powder, pepper, ginger, garlic, paprika, yoghurt, lemon juice and food colouring if being used. Pour this mixture over the cubed Paneer and leave to marinate for 10-12 hours - the longer the better.

Bake the Paneer, uncovered for 15 - 20 minutes at 220C, 425F, gas mark 7. Alternatively, put the Paneer onto skewers and barbecue.

Serves 2 (or 4 as a starter)

For further information please contact:
The Marketing Dept, Long Clawson Dairy Ltd, Long Clawson, Melton Mowbray, Leicestershire LE14 4PJ.   Telephone: 01664 822332   Fax: 01664 823236

Paneer Fried Rice

Ingredients

227g / ½lb Paneer (cut into 15mm cubes)
227g / ½lb Basmati Rice
100g / 4 oz frozen peas
1 onion, finely chopped
1 -2 (to taste) green chillies, finely chopped
1cm piece of ginger, chopped
½ teaspoon cumin seeds
½ teaspoon turmeric
½ teaspoon garam masala
½ teaspoon salt
200g / 8oz of tinned tomatoes
100g / 4oz cashew nuts
2 tablespoons oil
fresh coriander for garnish

Method

Soak the rice one hour before cooking.

Heat the oil in a large pan and cook the onions until soft. Add the ginger, tomatoes, chillies, spices and salt. Keep stirring, until most of the liquid has evaporated.

Add the cubed Paneer. Cover the pan and simmer on a low heat for 4 - 5 minutes. Make sure that the mixture does not stick.

Meanwhile, boil the rice (in a covered pan) in double its quantity of salted water for 10 - 12 minutes. Drain when cooked.

Mix together the rice, the Paneer mixture and the cashew nuts. Garnish with coriander and serve.

Serves 2 - 3

Palak Paneer

Ingredients

227g / ½lb Paneer cut into small cubes
butter or oil for frying
227g / ½lb fresh spinach
1 small onion
1 fresh tomato, skinned and chopped
1 clove garlic, crushed
small piece of fresh ginger, chopped
1 fresh green chilli, chopped
¼ teaspoon turmeric powder
½ teaspoon mixed spice
onion rings and tomato rings for garnish
salt and pepper to taste

Method

Heat some oil in a large pan. Fry the Paneer quickly until golden brown then put it to one side. Roughly chop the spinach leaves.

Using the same pan, fry the onion until golden brown then add the ginger, chilli and garlic. Cook for a further minute. Add the tomato, salt, pepper, turmeric and mixed spice. Cook until the oil sparates.

Add the spinach. Cover and cook on a low heat until the spinach is tender and the mixture is almost dry.

Add the Paneer, stir and cook for 5 minutes on a low heat. Add a small amount of hot water if too dry.

Garnish with onion rings and tomato rings. Serve with naan bread or rice.

Serves 2

Scrambled Paneer.

Can be used as a snack, starter or a side dish.

Ingredients

227g / ½lb Paneer, crumbled or grated
oil for frying
1 onion, finely chopped
2 green chillies, chopped
1 small piece of fresh ginger, chopped
2 chopped tomatoes
1 teaspoon chilli powder
1 teaspoon turmeric powder
salt to taste
fresh coriander to garnish

Method

Heat the oil in a frying pan and gently fry the onion for about 1 minute.

Add the green chillies and chopped ginger. Continue to fry for 1 minute.

Add the chopped tomatoes, chilli powder and turmeric. Continue cooking for 1 minute.

Stir in the Paneer and add salt to taste.

Cook for 1 - 2 minutes and serve hot, garnished with coriander leaves.

Serves 2 - 3

CCHI
dish

1 Heat the butter in a large pan, and gently cook the shallots.

2 Add the dry vermouth and half the double cream and bring to the boil. Season with a salt and pepper.

3 Add the spinach. The spinach will probably be spilling out from the pan, but don't worry because it will shrink down to nothing in a matter of seconds.

4 Add the rest of the cream, the cheese and the gnocchi, and stir well.

5 Pour the mixture into a gratin dish, and sprinkle with the breadcrumbs and Parmesan. Bake in a preheated oven at gas mark 6/200°C/ 400°F for 30 minutes.

CARBONARA

This a British favourite – however we tend to do it differently to the Italians. We like to add lots of double cream, whereas the Italians use beaten egg. I have used both.

serves 4-6

1 packet spaghetti
25 g/1 oz butter
4-5 rashers bacon, cut into pieces
½ glass dry vermouth
1 tablespoon olive oil
4 eggs, beaten
150 ml/¼ pint double cream
75 g/3 oz Parmesan, grated
1 bunch parsley, chopped
salt and freshly ground black pepper

1 Cook the spaghetti in a large pan of boiling, salted water, following the cooking time on the packet. Meanwhile, in a frying pan, melt the butter and then fry the bacon, until crisp. Add the dry vermouth.

2 Once the spaghetti has cooked, drain it and add it to the frying pan with the bacon. Add the olive oil, and season with salt and pepper, and then turn the heat off.

3 In a separate bowl, beat together the eggs and cream, and then add to the bacon, stirring continuously for 2-3 minutes. The eggs will cook with the heat of the pasta.

4 Stir in the Parmesan, and serve topped with the parsley.

Stir–fry cellophane
NOODLES with prawns

You can make this into a noodle soup by adding stock.

**serves 2
(as starter)**

**4 (as main
course)**

125 g/4 oz cellophane noodles

3 tablespoons vegetable oil

4 shallots, thinly sliced

2-3 slices ginger

2 cloves garlic, thinly sliced

6 slices fresh chilli

250 g/8 oz jumbo prawns,
shelled and de-veined

1 cup chicken or fish stock

1 tablespoon fish sauce
or soy sauce

2 spring onions, finely sliced

1 tablespoon freshly shredded
coriander leaves

1 Put the noodles in a large bowl and pour hot water over them to cover. Wait for 1-2 minutes, and then drain the noodles in a colander. When drained, plunge the noodles into ice cold water. Drain, and cut the noodles into pieces about 8 cm/3 in long.

2 Heat the oil in a wok or large pan and gently fry the shallots, ginger, garlic and chilli until the shallots start to colour.

3 Add the prawns and stir for 1 minute before adding the noodles, stirring to mix well.

4 Add the stock and fish or soy sauce. Stir for 1-2 minutes, until the noodles have absorbed most of the liquid.

5 Finally, stir in the spring onions. Serve scattered with the shredded coriander.

TIP
Be careful what you touch after handling chillies! You could wear rubber or plastic gloves, but a more practical way to protect your fingers is to rub your hands with cooking oil before touching chillies.

Grains & rice

Rice has always been a popular staple, and it is good to see more varieties becoming widely available. Have a good look in your local shops and you will see all the basics: short grain rice, pudding rice, basmati rice, and maybe some of the less well known: Arborio (risotto rice), flaked rice and jasmine rice. Manufacturers have realised that many people think they can't cook rice, so there is also a huge range of quick-cook, non-stick rices out there, and I'm happy about that. But I also want to show you how you can cook any kind of rice, and how it can be fluffy and delicious, and not one large, soggy mass.

Grains such as polenta, cracked wheat (bulgur wheat) and couscous are all wonderful ingredients, and I'm going to show you how to use these relative newcomers. Purists will tell you that polenta has to be cooked for 50 minutes of laborious stirring. Well, you can if you want to, but the 5-minute polenta that is available is fine for most recipes, so stick with that for an easy life. Some may argue that cracked and bulgur wheat are different things altogether, but they are pretty much the same in my book. Couscous is very easy to use, and can be boiled or steamed, just like rice.

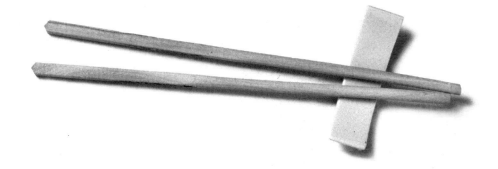

HOW TO COOK RICE

The basic rule is have twice as much
water as rice, so start with 2 cups of
water, to one cup of rice. Put the
rice and water into a large pan
and bring to the boil.
Simmer until the water
has disappeared, and
the rice will be cooked.
Alternatively, if you are a
little nervous of this method,
use a large pan with loads of water,
and cook your rice for 10-15
minutes (test a couple of grains after
10 minutes to see how it is coming
along). When you are happy it is
ready, rinse the rice in lots of hot water.
Leave to stand for a minute, then serve.

HOW TO COOK PILAU RICE

Proper pilau rice is done in the oven. It isn't
the yellowish rice you buy in bags, and boil.
There's nothing to it, so I suggest you try this
method, and save your money.

Again, use 2 parts of water to 1 part rice. Heat a
little oil in a large, heavy-based pan, and gently
cook some chopped onion and garlic. Add 1 cup of
rice, and stir to mix thoroughly. When mixed, tip
into a buttered casserole dish, and pour in 2 cups of
vegetable or chicken stock. Add 2 bay leaves and 2
sprigs of thyme, and cover with tin foil. Cook in a
preheated oven at gas mark 6/200°C/400°F for
15-20 minutes. The rice will absorb all the moisture,
and leave you with fluffy, delicious rice.

WARM RICE SALAD

Serving a salad warm really enhances the flavour of
the ingredients. Why not try mixing some freshly
cooked rice with some chopped spring
onions, mint, parsley, red peppers
and plum tomatoes? Whizz up a
quick salad dressing from olive
oil, lemon juice and salt and
pepper, and then mix
everything together. Ideal to
serve with some barbecued fish
or meat.

RISOTTO

Arborio rice is sometimes labelled as risotto rice in supermarkets – it's the same thing.

serves 4

1.2 litres/2 pints chicken stock
175 g/6 oz butter
1 onion, finely diced
1 clove garlic, diced
1 teaspoon soft thyme
300 g/10 oz Arborio rice
150 ml/¼ pint white wine
a selection of wild mushrooms, finely sliced
2 handfuls of spinach leaves
75 g/3 oz Parmesan, ground
salt and freshly grated black pepper

1 In a large saucepan, bring the stock to the boil. Meanwhile, melt 50 g/ 2 oz of the butter in a large frying pan. When the butter begins to froth, add the onion, garlic and thyme. Cook until the onion is soft but not brown.

2 Add the Arborio rice to the pan and stir thoroughly until combined with the onions and butter. Cook for a further 2 minutes then add the white wine. When that has been absorbed by the rice add a ladle of hot stock. Stir until the rice has absorbed the liquor and repeat, adding a small amount of stock at a time. Simmer for 15-20 minutes until the rice is nearly tender, but with a little bite.

3 In a separate frying pan, melt 50 g/2 oz of the butter, and fry the mushrooms gently for 4-5 minutes.

4 Five minutes before the end of cooking, add the mushrooms and the spinach to the rice. Stir in the Parmesan cheese and the remaining butter. Season to taste, and serve immediately.

RISOTTO cakes

Risotto cakes are a good way of adding a little crunch to risotto. You could also use leftover risotto, if you have made too much. Using cold risotto, roll and flatten handfuls of risotto into patties. Mix together some breadcrumbs and grated Parmesan cheese, and coat the patties in the mixture. Melt some butter in a large frying pan, and fry the patties until golden on both sides.

TABBOULEH

Cracked wheat is also
known as bulgur wheat.

serves 4

125 g/4 oz cracked wheat, soaked
for 10 minutes in cold water

2 large, ripe tomatoes, deseeded,
skinned and diced

1 small cucumber, diced

3 spring onions, finely sliced

large handful of flat leaf parsley,
chopped

large handful of mint, chopped

juice of 1 lemon

1 tablespoon olive oil

salt and freshly ground
black pepper

1 Drain the wheat through a sieve and then squeeze the wheat in your hand to get rid of any excess water.

2 Place the wheat in a bowl with the rest of the ingredients and combine them using your hands.

3 Season with salt and pepper and dribble with a little more olive oil, to serve.

RICE pudding

This is a recipe for a traditional, baked rice pudding, but you can also make this on a stovetop. Bring the milk and bay leaf to the boil in a large saucepan, and add the rice and sugar. Simmer gently for about ½ hour, until thick and creamy. Remove the bay leaf before serving.

serves 4

600 ml/1 pint milk

1 bay leaf

50 g/2 oz caster sugar

50 g/2 oz short grain rice, washed and drained

butter, for greasing

nutmeg, to grate

1 Heat the milk in a large saucepan with the bay leaf. When the milk is almost at the boil, take it off the heat, and add the sugar and rice. Stir until the sugar has melted.

2 Pour the pudding mixture into a medium-size, buttered baking dish and remove the bay leaf. I suggest you place the pie dish on a baking sheet before you pour in the milk, as this will make it easier to move, and will catch any spills. Grate the nutmeg over the top of the mixture and then place in a preheated oven at gas mark 3/170°C/325°F. Bake for 1-1½ hours or until a golden skin has formed over the top of the pudding.

SEAFOOD

Seafood

I think many people are put off preparing their own seafood by all the shells and legs and things, but it's very easy to prepare.

HOW TO COOK LOBSTER

To cook a lobster, place it in a large pan with salted, cold water. Bring to the boil. Some books recommend that you plunge a lobster in boiling hot water, but I think this makes it tough. I guess if you are cooking one live you might want to do this, but I think most of us will buy a dead one from the supermarket or fishmonger, so let's not worry about that. Don't add any vegetables or flavourings of any kind. Seafood should taste of the

sea, so just keep it simple. To prepare a lobster, you need a good, heavy knife, such as a butcher's knife. Break off the legs, and cut down the length of the body. Remove any part that doesn't look like white or grey meat. Lastly, prepare the claws by pulling off the shell to expose as much meat as possible, leaving a bit of claw to give you something to grip.

HOW TO COOK SCALLOPS

Don't waste your time with frozen scallops. The freezing process makes them watery, which makes them difficult to grill or fry. Frozen scallops are only OK if you are using them in a sauce. To open, slide a knife along the flat side of the shell. Cut out the scallop, and trim away the skirt.

& FISH

HOW TO COOK SQUID

Now that squid has become trendy we aren't afraid to call it squid – remember when it was called calamari? Now, it is, of course, possible to prepare and clean a squid yourself, but it's a messy and time-consuming job, so why not ask your friendly fishmonger to do it for you. They are happy to do it, for no extra cost.

Cooking squid is rather strange. The rule is, either cook for a very short time, or for a very long time – either for 1½ minutes, or for 1½ hours! Strange but true. To grill a squid, slice lengthways, and open the squid out. Slash the flesh ¾ of the way through. Grill for 45 seconds on each side – that's it! Or you can roast it for 1½ hours, wrapped in tin foil.

HOW TO PREPARE MUSSELS

To clean mussels, fill a bucket with water, and add a handful of flour. Add the mussels, and the flour somehow does the cleaning for you. Rinse well, and they are ready to cook. To 'debeard' mussels, use a knife to scrape towards the tail end of the shell.

HOW TO PREPARE PRAWNS

Treat raw and cooked whole prawns in the same way. Pull off the head and the tail, and peel the shell away, removing the legs with the shell. For large prawns, cut down the backbone, and remove the dark thread.

HOW TO OPEN OYSTERS

You can buy gadgets that help you with this, but the usual way is to place the oyster on a firm surface, on a towel, and insert a knife into the oyster shell. Twist the knife, to prise off the top shell.

MUSSELS
in coconut milk curry

The mussels are served in their shells, so you might like to have a bowl of water ready to clean your fingers. A good way to eat mussels is to eat one, then use its shell like a pair of tweezers to pick out the other mussels.

serves 4

1 tablespoon peanut oil

1 teaspoon Thai green curry paste

1 clove garlic, finely chopped

1 tablespoon finely chopped ginger

½ teaspoon ground turmeric

450 ml/¾ pint coconut milk

2 kaffir lime leaves

1 stalk lemongrass, finely chopped

32 mussels, bearded

2 teaspoons fish sauce

1 teaspoon sugar

1 tablespoon fresh lime juice

2 tablespoons freshly torn basil leaves

1 Heat the peanut oil in a medium frying pan and sauté the Thai green curry paste, garlic and ginger for 2 minutes.

2 Add the turmeric, coconut milk, lime leaves and lemongrass and simmer, uncovered, for about 5 minutes.

3 Add the mussels, cover, then increase the heat and cook for 5 minutes until the mussels have opened. Discard any that haven't opened, as they will be 'off'.

4 Add the fish sauce, sugar and lime juice and simmer for 1 minute, shaking the pan to mix the ingredients. Serve sprinkled with the basil.

PAELLA

Paella is the first dish recorded where meat and fish were cooked in the same dish. It was first made over 200 years ago in Valencia, and Paella Valenciana is still the region's most famous dish. It developed as a picnic dish; basically families cooked rice on Sunday outings, and threw in whatever they had, whether it was chicken, seafood or rabbit. I don't know if they actually went out and caught the extra ingredients themselves!

serves 4

2 tablespoons oil

1 shallot, peeled and sliced

2 cloves garlic, peeled and crushed

2 chicken thighs, cut into large chunks

250 g/8 oz paella rice

pinch of saffron strands, soaked in 2 tablespoons warm milk

600 ml/1 pint hot fish stock

125 g/4 oz fresh or frozen peas

125 g/4 oz prawns

3 large squid, bodies cut into rings

250 g/8 oz mussels, cleaned

125 g/4 oz clams

salt and freshly ground black pepper

1 Heat the oil in a large paella pan (or a large frying pan) and fry the shallot and garlic for 1 minute. Add the chicken and cook for 3 minutes until browned all over.

2 Add the rice, saffron strands and milk, stock and peas. Season with salt and freshly ground black pepper and bring to the boil.

3 Add the seafood, cover with foil and simmer for 20 minutes until the rice is tender, the chicken and squid cooked through and the shellfish opened. Stir to mix and serve immediately.

Fish

The UK seems scared of fish, but we seem happy to eat it in restaurants, perhaps because chefs will have taken the difficulty out of it.

Fish fashions change rapidly. Salmon was once very expensive, but demand has brought the price right down. Conversely, cod is being over-fished at the moment, so the price will go up. Monkfish is the trendy fish of the moment, whereas it used to be cheap, and thrown away.

To tell if a fish is fresh, look for the following:

❦ shiny, rounded eyes that are not sunken
❦ the gills should be red not pink
❦ the scales should be shiny, not dull
❦ the fish should smell of the sea, not of ammonia

HOW TO POACH A FISH

To poach cod or smoked haddock, place the fish in a large, heavy-based pan with 1.2 litres/2 pints of milk, an onion, a bay leaf, a few cloves, a sprig of thyme, a small bunch of parsley and some peppercorns. Bring to the boil and then allow to cool. When the milk has cooled, the fish will be done.

To poach trout or salmon, use *court bouillon* instead of milk, which is water with a sprig of thyme, a chopped bunch of spring onions, a chopped shallot, a chopped leek and some peppercorns. Again, bring to the boil with the fish, and then leave to cool.

HOW TO ROAST OR BAKE A FISH

You can bake fish in foil or paper (*en papillote*). Use a large piece of foil or paper, and lay the fish in the centre. Dribble over some white wine and lemon juice, add a knob of butter, some chopped dill, and/or chervil, and season with salt and pepper. You could also add a splash of Worcester sauce for a different flavour. Fold over the foil or paper and crumple at the top, ensuring the parcel has no open gaps, and leaving room inside the parcel for the steam to circulate. Bake in a preheated oven at gas mark 4/180°C/350°F for 25 minutes for a small fish, 35 for a large fish. Be careful when you open the parcel, as it is full of hot air.

HOW TO PAN-FRY FISH

Cover your piece of fish in seasoned flour. Heat some butter and oil in a large pan until it is very hot, and then place the fish in the pan, skin side down, to cook for 1 minute. Turn the fish over, and do the other side for 1 minute. Add some rock salt and a good squeeze of lemon or lime juice, and place the whole pan in a preheated oven at gas mark 4/180°C/350°F. Bake for 3-4 minutes. Serve with some of the pan juices, depending on whether you want to be health-conscious or not.

HOW TO DEEP-FRY FISH

Fried cod in batter is the best in the world, if it is lovely and crisp – soggy fish is horrid. But perfect fried fish is possible. Here's how:

You really need a deep-fat fryer for this, because you need to heat the oil to 180°C/350°F.

To make a batter, put 125 g/4 oz flour in a large mixing bowl, and make a well in the centre. Add 1 egg and a little milk and, using a wooden spoon, work the flour into the centre. Add milk until it forms a batter consistency. Add the grated rind and juice of 1 lemon, and season with salt and pepper. Beat 1 egg white until stiff, and then gently fold into the batter. Don't beat the batter; be gentle, and you will be rewarded with light, crispy batter.

Dip your fish in the batter. You could then dip it in flour for a different texture. For a thin piece of plaice, fry for 5 minutes. For a thicker piece of fish, such as cod, fry for about 10 minutes.

Roast MONKFISH

This is perfect for a special meal, but if you want to use this as an everyday recipe, you can replace the monkfish with a thick piece of cod. You could also make individual portions, so each person can open their own parcel. I think pancetta is best for this recipe, but you could also use Parma ham or streaky bacon.

serves 4

2 tablespoons olive oil

1 x 1 kg/2 lb monkfish tail

125 g/4 oz pancetta, thinly sliced

40 g/1½ oz butter

large bunch dill, chopped

large bunch parsley, chopped

small bunch chervil,chopped

2 shallots, finely chopped

salt and freshly ground
black pepper

1 Lay a large sheet of tin foil on a flat surface and dribble the olive oil over the surface. With your fingers, rub the oil all over the foil. Lay down the strips of pancetta, so that they overlap. Lay the monkfish on top.

2 Melt the butter, and gently fry the shallots. Plunge the dill, parsley and chervil into a small saucepan of boiling water for a few seconds, and then drain. Plunge into a bowl of iced water, and then whizz in a food processor. Spread the herb mixture along the length of the monkfish, and season.

3 Fold the pancetta around the monkfish, enclosing the herb mixture. Squeeze the foil tightly around the fish and then cook in a preheated oven at gas mark 4/ 350°F/180°C for 20-25 minutes. The fish should be firm to the touch when done. Undo the foil for the last 5 minutes, to allow the pancetta to brown slightly.

FISH cakes

I use a mixture of fish for this recipe, but you could use just one variety, and increase the quantity.

makes 12

250 g/8 oz salmon

200 g/7 oz cod

200 g/7 oz haddock

1.2 litres/2 pints milk

1 onion, chopped

75 g/3 oz butter

500 g/1 lb mashed potato

1 tablespoon anchovy essence

3 tablespoons chopped parsley

2 tablespoons chopped dill

1 medium egg

1 hard-boiled egg, chopped

breadcrumbs, to coat

salt and freshly ground black pepper

1 Poach the fish in the milk as directed on page 42. Meanwhile, fry the onion in 25 g/1 oz butter until soft.

2 Place the mashed potato in a bowl and mix in the drained, poached fish and onions. Next add the anchovy essence and chopped parsley and dill and mix. Season with salt and pepper to taste.

3 Beat the raw egg in a separate bowl, then add to the potato mix. Finally, add the hard-boiled egg.

4 Divide the mixture into 12, and roll each piece into a ball. Flatten gently with your hand to form a fish cake shape, and leave to chill in a fridge for at least 2 hours.

5 When chilled, cover the fish cakes in fine breadcrumbs. Melt the remaining butter in a large pan, and gently fry the fish cakes for 3 minutes on each side, or until golden brown. Drain and serve.

BREADCRUMBS

Breadcrumbs are extremely easy to make, and it baffles me why anyone would part with good money for those horrid breadcrumbs you can buy. Use any loaf of bread, and whizz it in a food processor (or grate if you don't have one) – simple. The bread can be a couple of days old.

CHIC

Free-range chickens have the best flavour. The yellow chickens you get have been fed on maize (sweetcorn). Guinea fowl is a cross between a pheasant and a chicken.

HOW TO PORTION A CHICKEN

Remove the legs and cut off the wings. Cut off the breasts, and cut down the centre through the chicken. Use the carcass for stock. Cut the leg in two to make a thigh and a drumstick.

HOW TO SAUTÉ CHICKEN

Mix together the lemon juice, olive oil, pepper and chilli, then place your choice of chicken pieces (breasts are ideal) in the mixture (a 'marinade'). You can coat the chicken in flour first if you like. (The healthiest way is not to coat in a flour crust, and simply to grill the chicken). Heat some oil or butter in a pan and fry the chicken for 6 minutes, and the chicken breasts for 4-5 minutes. Add some shredded sage, chopped tomatoes and a glass of wine and boil to a frenzy, until the liquid has reduced. Add a little salt and 50 g/2 oz butter and stir well. Serve the chicken in the cooking juices.

HOW TO STEAM CHICKEN

If you fancy a healthy chicken dish, try steamed, Chinese-style chicken. It's very easy, and delicious served with plain, boiled or steamed rice. Marinate some sliced chicken in soy sauce, lemon rind, garlic and ginger, and place in a steamer for 10-12 minutes. See page 34 for how to cook rice, and place your marinated chicken above it, so they cook at the same time. When both are cooked. add some chopped herb salt and pepper to the rice, and serve with the chicken placed on top.

KEN

HOW TO ROAST A CHICKEN

This is probably the favourite way of cooking a
chicken, and it is very simple. However, if you have
bought an average, factory-farmed chicken, you'll
need to add something to give it some extra flavour.
Mix 50 g/2 oz of butter, 50 g/2 oz cream cheese
with some chopped herbs, and smear under and
over the chicken skin, and tuck some more under
the skin, for extra moistness. This adds a lovely
flavour, and ensures that the chicken is well basted
and moist throughout cooking. Put a cut lemon, a
couple of sprigs of rosemary and a couple of cloves
of garlic inside the chicken. Place in a large baking
tray on a bed of root vegetables ('roots'), which
helps to prevent the chicken sticking to the tray,
and are delicious when roasted. Add a knob of lard
or dripping to the chicken and then roast for 20
minutes per 500 g/1 lb. Don't be tempted to cook
for an extra 20 minutes as some might suggest, else
you'll get a very tough old bird.

HOW TO BOIL A CHICKEN

You might be thinking – why on earth do you want
to boil a chicken? I agree, it sounds like a sure way
to get rid of any flavour the chicken might have. But
it's a very useful way to prepare chicken for use in
salads, sandwiches, curries and for recipes that have
very creamy sauces. Simply put the chicken, some
slices of root ginger and some chopped spring
onions into a large pan of boiling water and simmer
for 10 minutes. Then turn the heat off and leave the
pan for 45 minutes. Finally, drain the chicken and
plunge it into a large bowl of iced water.

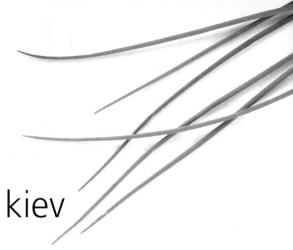

CHICKEN kiev

One of the most popular ways of cooking chicken, this is a boned chicken breast rolled around a chunk of herb butter. The breast is covered in breadcrumbs and fried until crisp. When pierced with a fork, the chicken should emit a jet of the fragrant butter.

serves 4

2 tablespoons fresh chopped chives

2 tablespoons fresh chopped flat-leaf parsley

1 large clove garlic, peeled and crushed

50 g/2 oz butter

1 teaspoon English mustard

4 skinless chicken breasts

plain flour

2 eggs, beaten

125 g/4 oz breadcrumbs

saffron rice to serve

1 In a small bowl, mix the chives and parsley with the garlic, butter and mustard to make a soft paste.

2 Lay the chicken breasts flat on a board and lightly flatten with a rolling pin. Lay a piece of clingfilm over each chicken breast and this time flatten the chicken with a little more force. Now you should have a nice flat surface on which to place the herb butter. Remove the clingfilm and spoon the herb butter along the middle of the chicken and then roll the chicken up lengthways.

3 Coat the chicken breast in flour, then the beaten egg and finally the breadcrumbs. Deep-fat fry the chicken kievs in a deep-fat fryer for 3-4 minutes. Remove, and drain on kitchen paper.

Opposite
Roast Monkfish (page 44).

Overleaf
Back: Beef Bourguignon (page 64), *Front*: Souvlakia (page 61).

Spicy CHICKEN pot roast

A spicy pot roast is an ideal way of giving your chicken dish a bit of a 'kick'. It's packed with loads of different fruits and vegetables, so it's a really healthy, nutritious option, full of wonderful flavours and very simple to cook.

serves 6

1.75 kg/4 lb corn-fed chicken

1-2 teaspoons harissa paste

1 teaspoon cumin

2 tablespoons olive oil

1 large onion, peeled, halved and cut into wedges

1 aubergine, trimmed and cut into large chunks

2 courgettes, trimmed and diagonally sliced into chunks

2 red peppers, halved, seeded and cut into large chunks

1 orange, thinly sliced

125 g/4 oz apricots

125 g/4 oz prunes

1 pint chicken stock

6 peppercorns

150 ml/¼ pint orange juice

1 bunch coriander, roughly chopped

salt

1 Rub the chicken all over with the harissa paste and cumin. Heat the oil in a large pan and add the chicken, breast side down. Sear all over for 2-3 minutes, until golden brown.

2 Place the chicken in a large roasting tray and add the onion, aubergine, courgettes, red peppers, orange slices, apricots, prunes, stock, peppercorns and orange juice. Pour over the chicken stock and season with plenty of salt.

3 Cover and cook in a preheated oven at gas mark 4/180°C/350°F for 1 hour. Garnish with coriander to serve.

GAME

RABBIT *stew if wild, or roast if farmed.*

PHEASANT *wonderful served with game chips and bread sauce.*

VENISON *farmed venison is red, fresh and vibrant, wild is grey and tougher.*

OSTRICH *now farmed in this country. It's very expensive for what it is, so I suggest you forget, unless for a one-off novelty.*

DUCK *mallard duck is very salty - good if roasted and stuffed with onion and lemon. This won't need hanging.*

WOODCOCK *this is the big brother of a snipe. Paul Bocuse said that snipe should fly through the oven, meaning that they should roast for just 8-10 minutes. You can eat every part of a woodcock's body - they have very clean innards, because, unlike most other birds, each time they take off, they go to the loo, so they are very clean inside!*

WOOD PIGEON *quite unlike the ones in Trafalgar square. The ones you can buy from your local butcher or supermarket are so cheap, you only need to use the really good bits. It mystifies me why people don't cook with them more, because they have a wonderful flavour, and are such good value. Why not try a warm salad of pigeon. Grill or fry the pigeons for 2 minutes on each side. Add a few fried lardons of bacon, wild mushrooms and croutons, and serve on some tasty salad leaves.*

QUAIL *a bit of a waste of space - they hardly have any meat. To spatchcock a quail, use scissors, as they are so small. Cut the bird either side of the backbone, and squash the pieces with the heel of your hand to flatten.*

HOW TO MARINATE AND COOK VENISON

Use 4 parts of wine/vinegar/citrus juice to 1 part of oil to make a marinade, which is the reverse of a dressing. Half the fun of dressings and marinades is to chuck in whatever you have to hand – I don't want you to get into measuring pedantically. Just use this rough ratio, and add whatever else you want. A marinade of port, red wine, red wine vinegar, olive oil, chopped garlic, chopped onion or shallots, sprig of thyme, bay leaf, chopped carrot and celery works well with venison. Marinate venison over night. To cook venison, treat like a piece of steak. Grill, griddle or fry for 2-3 minutes on each side, smeared with a little oil, rock salt and pepper. Reduce the marinade to make a sauce, and serve both with braised red cabbage.

HOW TO ROAST A GAME BIRD

Game birds are very leans, and therefore can dry out very easily during roasting. I suggest you wrap your birds in streaky bacon before roasting. The fat will melt onto the bird, and keep the meat tender. Roast at gas mark 5/190°C/375°F for 20 minutes per 500 g/1 lb for quail, and gas mark 4/180°C/350°F for 30 minutes for duck. Always leave a roast to stand for 10-15 minutes before carving, to let the meat relax, and become more tender.

Salmis of PHEASANT

Pheasants are shot in the wild – so they aren't very popular with animal rights people. But if you want to have a go at pheasant – here's how. You will need to hang your pheasant for 3-4 days.

serves 2

1 pheasant, plucked, gutted and washed, claws cut off

bed of vegetables, i.e. carrots, potatoes, turnips, celery

125 g/4 oz streaky bacon, diced

6-8 juniper berries

1 bottle red wine

1 tablespoon tomato purée

400 g/14 oz tinned, chopped tomatoes

1 tablespoon redcurrant jelly

1 Roast the pheasant in a large roasting tray on a bed of root vegetables covered with the bacon and juniper berries. This will take 25 minutes in a preheated oven gas mark 7/220°C/425°F.

2 Remove the roasting tin from the oven and lift out the pheasant and place carefully on a board. Place the roasting tin on a gas hob and pour a little red wine into the tin. Using a wooden spoon, scrape the sides of the tin to extract all the juices from the pheasant, and stir the vegetables into the wine to fully combine the flavours.

3 Cut the meat off the thighs and breasts of the bird, but not the drumsticks, as they are very sinewy. Use a heavy knife to chop up the pheasant carcass into fine shreds. Place the shreds into the roasting tin with the vegetables, as this will later make the gravy. Stir the bones around to combine the flavours

in the tin and then pour the contents into a saucepan and heat gently.

4 Add the tomato purée, chopped tomatoes, redcurrant jelly and the rest of the bottle of wine. Simmer for 15-20 minutes and top up from time to time using a little chicken stock.

5 Sieve the stock to remove all the bones and vegetables, and then reheat in a clean pan to reduce to gravy consistency.

6 Remove the skin from the thighs and breasts of pheasant and add to the sauce to heat through. Serve the pheasant sliced, with potatoes and boiled red cabbage.

QUAIL with coconut

Quail is a white meat with a delicate flavour and can be cooked in the same way as other game. Young birds can be roasted or fried, and older fowl should be cooked with moist heat. Coconut is an ideal accompaniment to the subtle taste of quail.

serves 2

1 teaspoon salt

2 teaspoons chopped garlic

1 teaspoon coriander powder

1 teaspoon cardamom pods

1 teaspoon fresh ginger

50 g/2 oz butter, melted

2 quails, spatchcocked
(see page 50)

2 tablespoons vegetable oil

2 tablespoons chopped
spring onion

1 teaspoon cumin

1 teaspoon chopped coriander

3 tablespoons desiccated coconut

1 teaspoon black pepper

olive oil

large bag of green salad

1 Grind the salt, 1 teaspoon of the chopped garlic, the coriander powder and cardamom pods together in a pestle and mortar. Add the ginger and melted butter and crush to form a paste.

2 Smear the quails with the paste and leave to marinate for at least ½ hour.

3 Heat the vegetable oil in a large pan and add the remaining garlic, the spring onion, cumin, chopped coriander and desiccated coconut. Season with black pepper and cook until the coconut is toasted brown.

4 Dribble some olive oil over a hot griddle pan and place the quails, paste side down, on the griddle. Cook on each side for 3-4 minutes to have the quails rare or 4-5 minutes to have them well done.

5 Place the quails on a bed of green salad and dribble over extra olive oil. Sprinkle over the coconut mixture and serve.

PORK

Just as brown is the new black, believe it or not, pork is fast becoming the new chicken. Forget what you've have been told about pork being fatty and unhealthy; it can be very lean. The bacon sandwich is actually quite good for you, as long as you grill the bacon, and avoid lashings of butter. One rasher is just 40 calories, so feel free to indulge yourself on a Sunday morning. Even a large pork chop or a few slices of roast pork are low in fat – as long as you trim off the skin and fat after cooking. I don't suppose many of you are going to be converted to the virtues of pig's trotters and pig's snouts etc. but there are plenty of other porky parts that are delicious and underused.

If you're feeling adventurous, roast some ribs in a barbecue sauce – very simple, so there's no need to cheat and buy a packet of barbecued ribs from the shops. Pork fillet is delicious, and underused. It's an ideal cut for kebabs, stir-fries and curries. And boiled bacon's tasty too, and a good alternative to a traditional roasted Sunday joint.

Knuckles of pork (sometimes called hock) are sold on the bone, or can be stuffed if your butcher is happy to bone them for you. They are generally used in sausages.

Bacon and ham are pig meats that have been cured. Ham is the cured hind leg of a pig, smoked, or salted and smoked. Bacon requires just 4-5 days curing, ham considerably longer.

HOW TO ROAST PORK

Leg, loin and shoulder of pork are all suitable cuts for roasting.

If the skin has already been removed, score a diamond pattern in the fat with a boning knife, baste with a little oil and rub with salt and pepper or a dry spice mix such as cinnamon, mustard powder and brown sugar.

Place the joint on a rack in a roasting tin and roast until well done.

HOW TO MAKE CRACKLING

A succulent joint of roast pork is delicious, but incomplete without crackling. It's pure fat and calories, but worth it! If you're feeling virtuous and decide to forfeit the crackling, then make sure you baste the joint with the fat from the tin every 30 minutes.

Place your joint on a rack in a roasting tray, and pour boiling water over the skin 2-3 times. Place in a fridge overnight. Just before cooking, pour cider vinegar over the joint (this won't flavour it) and then cover liberally with salt. Roast in the normal way.

HOW TO BOIL BACON

Most joints of bacon from the supermarket or butcher's have been pre-soaked – ask if you feel unsure. If not, you'll need to soak it yourself, to prevent the meat tasting salty. It's a simple process but a bit of a chore. Soak the bacon overnight, preferably under a dripping tap, so the water flows away from the joint, taking with it any salt. In the morning, place the joint in a clean, large pan of fresh water, and bring to the boil. Boil for just a minute or two, and then change the water. This process sweet-cures the meat.

To cook the bacon, add chunks of onion, carrot and celery, a bay leaf, a few parsley stalks, cloves and black peppercorns, and bring to the boil. Boil for 20 minutes for each 500 g/1 lb of meat, skimming off any scum that floats to the top (the scum is salt). When cooked, cut the rind off, and slice the bacon. Serve with Colcannon, cabbage, carrots, onions and parsley sauce for a truly Irish experience. And don't throw the cooking water away; it makes wonderful stock for pea and ham soup.

Spare ribs

An ideal, sweet starter. Here we're making American ribs, rather than Chinese-style.

serves 3-4

2 tablespoons olive oil
1 medium onion, finely sliced
1 clove garlic, finely chopped
1 tablespoon fennel seeds
1 chilli, finely sliced
250 g/8 oz soft brown sugar
150 ml/¼ pint soya sauce
600 ml/1 pint tomato ketchup
6 tablespoons water
10 large, meaty spare ribs

1. Heat the olive oil in a large saucepan, and gently fry the onions and garlic until softened but not coloured.

2. Add the fennel seeds, chilli, sugar and soya sauce. Turn the heat up and stir in the tomato ketchup and water. Heat through for 2-3 minutes.

3. Add the spare ribs and stir until the ribs are well coated in the sauce. Turn the heat down and simmer for approximately 1½ hours, until the meat is tender.

4. Remove the ribs from the saucepan and skim off the fat from the sauce with a ladle. Reheat the sauce, stirring well, and pour the sauce over the ribs to serve.

Irish PORK in Stout with Spices

A hearty main course using knuckles of pork and flavoured with the essential Irish nectar!

serves 4

2 knuckles of pork

6 sage leaves

6 black olives

6 anchovy fillets

6 prunes

175 g/6 oz brown sugar

65 g/2½ oz butter

2 tablespoons olive oil

1 onion, sliced

1 bottle of stout such as Guinness or Murphy's

15 g/½ oz plain flour

1 clove garlic

1 tablespoon chopped oregano

small bunch thyme

1 tablespoon vinegar

2 teaspoons salt

2 teaspoons freshly ground black pepper

1 To prepare the knuckles, slice the rind off the pork and reserve to one side. Make six cuts in each knuckle.

2 Wrap a sage leaf around each olive and insert into half the incisions. Wrap an anchovy fillet around each prune and insert in the remaining holes.

3 In a blender, mix together the brown sugar, garlic, oregano, thyme, vinegar, salt and pepper to form a paste. Smear over the knuckles and leave overnight in a fridge to marinate.

4 Melt 50 g/2 oz butter and olive oil in a large frying pan and brown the knuckles for about 8 minutes, turning until the meat is browned all over.

5 Add the onion, the marinade and the stout, and stir well until the meat is well coated, and the sauce is bubbling gently. Transfer everything to a roasting tray.

6 Place the rind that you removed from the knuckles back on top of the meat, and then place the roasting tray in a preheated oven at gas mark 1/130°C/ 250°F for 3½ hours.

7 To serve, remove the rind, and remove the knuckle bones. Place the meat in a heated serving dish.

8 Pour the cooking juices into a blender and whizz until smooth. Strain, and then reheat in a clean saucepan.

9 In a bowl, mix together the flour and remaining butter, and stir into the sauce to thicken. Pour the sauce over the meat. Serve immediately.

LAMB

I don't think you can beat a roasted leg of lamb – if you can buy lamb early in spring, when the legs are small and tender, it tastes truly fantastic. Sweet and succulent, what better way is there to herald the coming of spring? To ring the changes, try neck fillets, which are a perfect size for kebabs and casseroles. Chump chops make a very easy meal – simply grill and serve with seasonal vegetables. For something a little more elegant, try 'French trimmed' cutlets. Look for cutlets with pale flesh, to get a young, tender meat ideal for simple grilling. As a general rule, the pinker the flesh, the younger the meat; red lamb is mutton. If you like strong tasting meat, try casseroling mutton for a tasty, rich substantial dish. When shopping for lamb, choose cuts that are surrounded by creamy white fat; yellow fat is a sign that the meat is past its best.

Lamb shanks (the area around the shin of the meat) are used in casseroles and stews. You should go for cuts with white bone and creamy white tissue.

HOW TO ROAST LAMB

I would use a leg of lamb for this, but you could try a best end of neck, or a breast of lamb. Slash the skin of the lamb and stuff pieces of rosemary, anchovy and garlic into the cuts. Don't be alarmed by the anchovy! You can't actually taste the fish, but it does add a wonderful salty flavour. It also melts away, so you won't even see it. Place the lamb in a roasting tray on a bed of root vegetables. Drizzle olive oil over the lamb and season liberally with freshly ground rock salt and black pepper. Roast in a preheated oven at gas mark 8/230°C/450°F for 10 minutes, then gas mark 5/190°C/ 375°F for 25 minutes per 500 g/1 lb if you like your lamb medium, and at gas mark 8/230°C/450°F for 10 minutes, then gas mark 5/190°C/ 375°F for 18 minutes per 500 g/1 lb if you like your lamb rare. Lamb should never be well done.

HOW TO GRILL LAMB

A grill is fine for cooking lamb, but I would recommend you buy a griddle pan. You use it to cook on the hob, so it is easier to work with. You only need to use a small amount of oil, and you get really attractive seared markings on the meat. Place your cutlets or chump chops on a hot, preheated grill, or drizzle a little olive oil over a hot griddle pan. Cook cutlets for 2-3 minutes each side, and chump chops for 3-4 minutes.

LAMB FOR SPECIAL OCCASIONS

You have probably seen a crown roast of lamb, or a guard of honour, and thought: 'there is absolutely no way I could ever make that'. I thought I would take you through what they actually are, to help take away the mystique.

A rack of lamb is one side of a lamb's ribcage. There are usually 6-9 cutlets in a rack. A crown roast is simply when you tie one or two racks of lamb together, to form a crown shape. To make the rack pliable, cut the membranes between each rib, then bend round, and tie to secure. Stuff the centre of the crown with a stuffing or filling of your choice. You can make a guard of honour by interlocking two racks like swords. You don't need

to tie them together; simply push hard together. A butcher will happily make a crown or a guard's honour for you, but you will probably need to order one in advance. Roast in the same way as a joint of lamb (see opposite).

I wouldn't bother buying those little, paper, frilly crowns. Best to leave the joint as it is, or garnish it with roasted apple wedges, drizzled with a little honey. I suggest you present the finished cooked joint to your guests, to show off your handiwork, then remove the joint to the kitchen to carve, as it can be quite hard work, and will probably fall apart at the first cut!

LAMB SHANKS
with garlic, rosemary & flageolet beans

This is my version of a French bistro dish 'Gigot d'Agneau'.
In Burgundy, it is flavoured further with juniper.

serves 4

2 lamb shanks

6 tinned anchovies, cut in half

12 small rosemary sprigs

12 slivers garlic

50 g/2 oz butter or dripping

2 carrots, roughly chopped

2 celery stalks, roughly chopped

1 leek, roughly chopped

1 onion, roughly chopped

1 bulb garlic, broken up
into cloves

1 sprig thyme

1 sprig rosemary

1 bay leaf

½ bottle red wine

300 ml/½ pint chicken/lamb
stock (optional)

FOR THE SAUCE

2 tablespoons olive oil

125 g/4 oz streaky bacon, cut into
small pieces

½ carrot, finely diced

a few stalks of celery, finely diced

½ onion, finely diced

6 cloves garlic, peeled

2 sprigs thyme

2 sprigs rosemary, chopped

4 tomatoes

400 g/13 oz tinned
flageolet beans

salt and freshly ground
black pepper

1 Start by preparing the
lamb shanks. Remove
the fat from the shanks, and
make 6 deep incisions in each
shank. Wrap a piece of
anchovy and rosemary around
each sliver of garlic, and
insert in each cut. Season
well with salt and freshly
ground black pepper.

2 Melt the butter or
dripping in a large
frying pan and brown the
shanks all over for 2-3
minutes. Remove the shanks
from the pan and place in a
large roasting dish.

3 Add the roughly
chopped carrots, celery,
leek, onion, garlic and herbs to
the frying pan and fry until the
vegetables are lightly browned.
Scoop the vegetables out and
add to the roasting dish.

4 Add the red wine to the
pan and 'deglaze', which
is to reduce the liquid at a
high heat. Make sure you
scrape all the residue from the
bottom of the pan – it all adds
to the flavour! Add to the
roasting dish.

5 Pour the chicken stock into the roasting dish and stir well. Cover and cook in a preheated oven at gas mark 1/140°C/275°F for 2½ hours.

6 Meanwhile, make the sauce. Heat the olive oil and gently fry the bacon. Add the finely diced carrot, celery, onion and garlic and cook until the vegetables have softened. Add the thyme, rosemary, tomatoes and flageolet beans and stir well until heated through. Set aside until the lamb is cooked.

7 When the lamb has finished cooking, remove the two lamb shanks to a casserole dish and keep warm. Whizz the cooking juices in a blender or food processor until smooth and then sieve. Stir into the bean sauce and transfer to a clean saucepan. Simmer gently for ½ hour.

8 Season the sauce to taste and then pour over the lamb. Return to the oven and reheat for 10 minutes.

SOUVLAKIA

This is great snacking food, and ideal for summer barbecues.

 **serves 2**

½ onion, grated

3 cloves garlic

1 teaspoon ground cumin

½ teaspoon cayenne pepper

4 tablespoons olive oil

250 g/8 oz lamb fillets, cut into 1 cm/½ in slices

2 pitta breads

juice of ½ lemon

4 tablespoons Greek yoghurt

½ teaspoon chopped mint leaves

½ teaspoon chopped coriander leaves

3 spring onions, sliced

salt and freshly ground black pepper

1 Mix together the onion, garlic, cumin, cayenne pepper and olive oil to make a marinade. Season liberally. Pour the marinade over the lamb and mix well to coat. Leave to marinate for a few hours – overnight is ideal.

2 Heat a heavy bottomed frying pan or griddle over a fierce heat. Don't add any oil, as there's plenty in the marinade. Cook the lamb in the pan for about 5 minutes, tossing frequently. Or skewer the lamb and grill or barbecue for 2 minutes each side.

3 Warm the pitta breads in a toaster and cut the top off each pitta to form a pocket. Stuff the lamb into the pocket and dribble with the lemon juice and yoghurt. Sprinkle over the chopped mint leaves, coriander and spring onion, and push the filling into the pockets. Eat immediately.

BEEF

Different cuts of beef are good for different recipes. We're all familiar with the cuts available for a straightforward steak: fillet, sirloin and rump. Fillet is the most tender, and most expensive, but for a really tasty steak, opt for rump every time; you get a much better flavour. If you want beef for casseroles and steak and kidney pies, opt for braising, chuck or skirt. They're tougher cuts than the steak cuts, but casseroles and pies have a lengthy cooking time. All have an excellent flavour; choose the one that seems a good buy on the day. The best joint for roasting is a rib of beef, but sadly this cut on the bone is no longer available to us. Sirloin is an alternative. Choose one that's deep, dark red in colour, with an even marbling of fat throughout. Topside and silverside are ideal for boiling or pot roasting, but not fatty enough for roasting.

HOW TO ROAST BEEF

For best results, remove your joint from the fridge two hours before cooking. Preheat your oven to gas mark 4/180°C/350°F. Put a large knob of dripping or lard in your roasting tray, and heat it on the hob, until the dripping sizzles. Season the beef with freshly ground black pepper and sear on both sides for 2 minutes. Remove from the pan, throw in a selection of root vegetables, and place the beef on top. Melt some more dripping or lard in a frying pan, and add a large glass of red wine. Stir until the fat is melted and then pour over the beef. Roast your joint of beef for 20 minutes per 500 g/1 lb, plus an extra 20 minutes.

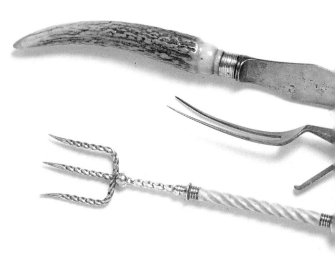

HOW TO MAKE YORKSHIRE PUDDING

Some people really fear Yorkshire pudding, and resort to those dreadful packet mixes you can buy. There's really no need. For a cheaper, tastier alternative to the packet, use an equal measure of eggs, plain flour and milk. If you use a cup each of eggs, flour and milk you will have enough batter for 4 large Yorkshire puddings. Sieve the flour into a large mixing bowl and add the eggs. Beat vigorously. Add the milk and season with salt and freshly ground black pepper. Beat well. If you have any lumps, sieve the batter. Leave the batter to rest for ½ an hour. Meanwhile, half fill each cup in your baking sheet with vegetable oil and heat in a preheated oven at gas mark 6/200°C/400°F. When piping hot, pour in the batter to fill the cups and cook for 25 minutes.

HOW TO GRILL STEAK

The trick to a delicious steak is to seal it in a hot frying pan, even if you are grilling it. This keeps the juices in the middle of the steak. Simply heat a drizzle of olive oil or knob of butter in a pan, and when hot, add the steak until it starts to colour. Sear on both sides. You could continue to fry the steak, but I think grilling produces the better flavour, and is slightly more healthy. If you add salt cook the steak immediately as salt draws the moisture out of the steak and makes it tougher.

For a rare steak, grill for just 2 minutes on each side. I wish those of you who only eat steak that is practically burnt to a cinder would try it rare sometime. If you don't like the sight of blood, wear a blindfold. I guarantee you'll love the flavour. But, if you're not convinced, grill for 3 minutes on each side for medium-rare, 4 minutes on each side for medium and 5-6 minutes on each side for well done. Cooking time varies according to thickness, so keep an eye on it. Steak is wonderful served with a little anchovy or herb butter.

ASIAN BEEF SALAD

Combine a dash each of light soy sauce, fresh lime juice and fish sauce; 1 chopped garlic clove; 1 diced chilli; a teaspoon of sugar; a finely sliced red and yellow pepper; a diced red onion and a sliced spring onion and toss through a few slices of rare beef. Garnish with lots of freshly chopped coriander leaves.

BEEF bourguignon

This is a delicious dish – the beef literally melts in your mouth.

serves 6

plain flour, for coating

1.5 kg/3½ lb blade or chuck beef steak, cut into 5 cm/2 in cubes

2 tablespoons olive oil

200 g/7 oz streaky bacon, cut into small pieces

12 small onions or 24 shallots, peeled

3 cloves garlic, finely chopped

2 glasses red wine

1 teaspoon tomato purée

1 teaspoon anchovy essence or Worcester sauce

2-3 stalks parsley

1 sprig thyme

1 bay leaf

18 small flat mushrooms

300 ml/½ pint well-flavoured meat stock

salt and freshly ground black pepper

chopped parsley, to serve

1 Season the flour and then sprinkle over the diced beef to cover thoroughly.

2 Heat the olive oil in a large frying pan and add some salt and freshly ground black pepper. Add the beef and fry gently for a few minutes until just browned. As each piece of beef becomes brown, remove it from the frying pan and reserve to one side.

3 Pour out most of the fat from the frying pan and add the bacon, onions or shallots and garlic, and cook gently for 3-4 minutes. Add the red wine, stirring well, and bring to the boil.

4 Return the meat to the pan and add the tomato purée and anchovy essence or Worcester sauce. Mix well and transfer everything to a large casserole dish.

5 Tie the parsley and thyme into a bundle using the bay leaf to make a bouquet garni. Add it to the casserole dish with the mushrooms. Pour over the stock and place in a preheated oven at gas mark 4/180°C/ 350°F. Cook for a minimum of 2 hours, but you can cook it for up to 8 hours – the longer the cooking time, the more tender the meat.

6 If you need to thicken the sauce before serving, remove the beef and pour the liquid into a large saucepan. Bring to the boil until the sauce thickens. Return the beef to the saucepan to heat through, and serve garnished with chopped parsley.

Opposite

Back: Salmis of Pheasant (page 52), *Front:* Chicken Kiev (page 48).

Overleaf

Back: Chargrilled Vegetable Lasagne (page 74), *Front:* Borscht (page 79).

MINCE & OFFAL

Mince

I've separated mince from the meat chapters, as I found there was so much I wanted to say about it that it made a programme in its own right. Mince is so versatile and easy to use that I couldn't do it justice tacked onto the end of the other programmes. You can mince any type of meat, but the ones we are most familiar with are lamb, pork and, of course, beef. Give pork mince a go – it's very good value and very low in fat. Pork mince is ideal for a recipe such as chilli con carne, and a good alternative to beef. Why not keep a pot of cooked mince in the freezer to use on its own or in a recipe? I've given you some ideas over the next few pages.

HOW TO MAKE SAVOURY MINCE

Use 500 g/1 lb of mince, and season with salt and freshly ground black pepper. If you are making this mince recipe ahead of cooking, add the salt just beforehand, to draw out moisture. Add ½ teaspoon of English mustard, a dash of Worcester sauce, a good pinch of chopped parsley, chives, and half an onion, finely chopped. You can gently fry the onion first for a couple of minutes to soften it. Gently fry all the ingredients until the mince is golden brown.

HOW TO MAKE BURGERS

Bind together 500 g/1 lb of savoury mince using 1 egg yolk. Get your hands into the mixture and give it a good mix. You can miss out the egg if you like a looser burger mix. Shape the mixture into burgers. Coat in seasoned flour and then shallow fry for 2-3 minutes on each side for a rare burger and 4-5 minutes for a medium burger. For a delicious adult version, shape with a dip in the middle and add a knob of butter and a piece of gorgonzola . Wrap the burger mixture around it, and cook as above. Serve in a toasted burger bun with plenty of lettuce, tomatoes and onion rings.

MOUSSAKA

Moussaka is a Greek dish, that we are quite familiar with, but I thinkit is rare to find it made well. Salting the aubergine is vital, as is the inclusion of nutmeg.

serves 6-8

FOR THE MEAT SAUCE

4 tablespoons olive oil

4 onions, chopped

5 cloves garlic, chopped

250 g/8 oz bacon, cut into small pieces

4 large carrots, chopped

4 sticks celery, chopped

2 bay leaves

3 sprigs thyme

1 teaspoon anchovy essence or Worcester sauce

2 teaspoons oregano

a pinch of nutmeg

750 g/1½ lb minced pork

750 g/1½ lb minced beef

1 bottle full-bodied red wine

75 g/3 oz tomato purée

2 x 400 g/13 oz tin chopped tomatoes

1.2 litres/2 pints of water

FOR THE CHEESE SAUCE

600 ml/1 pint milk

1 onion studded with a bay leaf and clove

50 g/2 oz butter

50 g/2 oz flour

75g/3 oz Gruyère, grated

2 medium eggs

4 small aubergines

flour, for coating

2 tablespoons breadcrumbs

2 tablespoons Parmesan, grated

salt and freshly ground black pepper

1 To make the meat sauce, heat half the olive oil in a large frying pan and fry the onions and garlic until softened, but not brown. Add the bacon, carrots, celery, bay leaves and thyme and cook for a further 5-6 minutes until the carrots start to soften. Then add the anchovy essence or Worcester sauce, oregano and nutmeg.

2 Meanwhile, in a separate pan, heat the remaining olive oil and gently fry the minced pork, turning to make sure all the mince is cooked. When brown, add to the vegetable mixture, being careful to leave some fat in the frying pan.

3 Pour the wine into the mixture, and stir well. Simmer gently. Meanwhile, cook the beef mince in the frying pan used to cook the pork. When brown, add to the main pan.

4 Add the tomato purée, tomatoes and water and stir well. Bring to the boil, then turn the heat down and simmer for 2 hours.

5 To make the cheese sauce, gently heat the milk in a large saucepan. Add the onion and simmer for about 20 minutes at a very low heat, then remove from the heat and remove the onion.

6 Melt the butter in a pan and add the flour. Stir constantly over a medium heat for 1 minute and then beat it into the milk. Return the milk to the hob and cook for 3-4 minutes, stirring constantly until the sauce is thick and smooth.

7 Take the pan off the heat and stir in the cheese. Stir until melted, then add the eggs and mix well.

8 To assemble the moussaka, place the aubergine slices in a colander and sprinkle with salt. Leave for an hour. This process removes any bitterness from the aubergine.

9 Rinse the aubergine and dip in flour until lightly coated. Shallow fry in olive oil until golden brown and drain on absorbent kitchen paper.

10 Divide the cheese sauce into two, and stir half of the cheese sauce into the meat sauce.

11 In a large baking dish, place a layer of aubergine, then a layer of meat sauce and pour over some of the remaining cheese sauce. Repeat until all the ingredients are used, ending with a thick layer of cheese sauce.

12 Mix the Parmesan and breadcrumbs together and then sprinkle over the moussaka. Cook in a preheated oven at gas mark 5/190°C/ 375°F for 45 minutes until golden brown and bubbling.

Kofta MEATBALLS

Meatballs have come a long way since I used to eat them at school! These meatballs are delicious, and are very useful for a number of dishes. I like to serve them stuffed into warmed pitta breads, filled with salad. For a more substantial meal, serve them with a good tomato sauce (you could just heat up some passata).

serves 4

500 g/1 lb lamb or beef, finely minced

1 onion, finely chopped

2 teaspoons ground cumin

1 teaspoon ground spice

pinch of cayenne pepper

handful of chopped coriander leaves

flour, for coating

4 tablespoons olive oil

salt and freshly ground black pepper

1 Blend all the ingredients, except the oil and flour, in a food processor until smooth and well-mixed.

2 Using your hands, take a small handful of the mixture and roll it into a ball. Repeat until you have used all the mixture. It might help to wet your hands before you do this, to prevent the mixture from sticking to your skin.

3 Roll the meatballs in flour until coated and then shallow fry the meatballs until they are golden brown. Drain on absorbent kitchen paper and serve.

Offal

'Offal' is a very off-putting word, and I know the word 'liver' puts people off even more, but it's time to banish the memory of horrid school liver. Pan-fried liver is all the rage now, and for good reason. Ox liver is the cheapest, but increasingly hard to find and too powerful for grilling or pan frying. Go for lamb's or calves liver instead. Calves is the best and dropping in price as demand rises. For pâté, buy chicken liver – affordable, and with a lovely flavour.

For kidney recipes use either pig's or lamb's kidneys, but I suggest you always soak them in milk first to remove any bitterness. Fresh lamb's kidneys come wrapped in suet, which you will have to peel away first.

HOW TO COOK LIVER

Unless you have a very good grill, it's best to fry liver. Cook the liver quickly at a very high temperature so the centre is still slightly pink. You could simply fry some chopped onions in butter with a little salt and sugar. Dip the liver in seasoned flour, add to the pan and cook until golden brown. For a truly British dish, serve with mashed potatoes, fried bacon and onions. For the Italian slant, add a dash of balsamic vinegar, chopped rosemary and serve with grilled vegetables or salad.

An all-time favourite breakfast of mine is kidney, bacon and mushroom on toast. Here's how: Melt a little butter in a large pan and start to fry 2 large field mushrooms on a gentle heat. Lay 2 rashers of bacon over the mushrooms and place the pan under a hot grill for about 5 minutes. Turn the bacon halfway through the cooking time. Meanwhile, soak 6 lamb's kidneys in milk, and slice in half. Remove the piece of white fat in the centre. Add the kidneys to the pan and return to the hob for a further 4 minutes, or until kidneys are golden brown and the bacon crispy. Serve piled on top of plenty of hot, buttered toast.

OX LIVER & bacon hotpot

If you are one of those people who claim to hate liver, try this, and prepare to change your mind!

serves 4-6

1 tablespoon flour

500 g/1 lb ox liver, cut into ½ cm/ ¼ in slices

125 g/4 oz streaky bacon, cut into small pieces

3 onions, sliced

1 carrot, cut into chunks

1 celery stalk, cut into chunks

50 g/2 oz swede, cut into chunks

1 teaspoon dried sage

600 ml/1 pint stock or water

1 teaspoon Worcester sauce

1 kg/2 lb potatoes, peeled and cut into fairly thick slices

melted beef dripping or butter

salt and freshly ground black pepper

1 Season the flour with salt and freshly ground black pepper, and toss the slices of liver in the flour to coat them well. Place in a large casserole dish and sprinkle over any remaining flour.

2 Add the bacon and sliced onion, together with the carrot, celery and swede. Add the sage and season with salt and pepper.

3 Pour in just enough stock or water to cover the ingredients in the casserole (probably about 600 ml/1 pint), and add the Worcester sauce.

4 Cover the top with the potatoes, overlapping each other, then season again with salt and pepper. Cover the casserole dish and cook in a preheated oven at gas mark 3/160°C/325°F for 2 hours. After that, remove the lid and cook for a further 30 minutes.

5 When you remove the casserole, brush the potatoes with a little melted beef dripping or butter and place the casserole under a hot grill until the potatoes are golden brown.

CHICKEN LIVER pâté

This is delicious served with plenty of hot, buttered toast.

serves 6-8

625 g/1¼ lb chicken livers (to make 500 g/1 lb when trimmed and cleaned)
200 g/7 oz softened butter
2 tablespoons brandy
1 teaspoon freshly grated nutmeg
salt and freshly ground black pepper

1 Cut away any green parts and threads from the liver; be thorough, as the tiniest amount left will make the pâté bitter.

2 Melt 1 tablespoon of the butter in a large frying pan and add half of the livers. Cook over a medium heat until golden brown all over. Remove the cooked livers to a plate. Add another tablespoon of butter and cook the remaining livers in the same way until golden brown.

3 Return the first batch of livers to the pan and increase the heat. Stir well, and then pour in the brandy. Ignite the brandy with a match and tilt the pan to spread the flaming brandy.

4 Season to taste with salt, freshly ground black pepper and the grated nutmeg, and mix well. Transfer to a food processor and blend until smooth.

5 Add the remaining butter and whizz again. Check the seasoning and serve.

VEGE

Green vegetables

Vegetables in Britain have changed over the past few years, and not necessarily for the better. The big supermarkets have made it possible for us to buy almost any kind of vegetable, at any time of the year. With world export and hi-tech growing techniques, vegetables are no longer seasonal. But I believe that if you buy vegetables in their natural season (when they are more widely available and cheaper), then you get better value for taste and money. If you have a spare bit of garden, why not try growing your own? It's extremely easy, and the results are sensational.

I'm not dazzled by the fashion for baby versions of vegetables. In my experience, they seem to have reduced flavour, to go with their reduced size. Likewise this growing demand for perfectly shaped veggies – are we really so squeamish that we can't eat knobbly potatoes? Is it really worth the extra dose of chemicals you get with them? Anyway, enough lecturing.

The Brits have come a long way since the advent of the boiled potato. There are simply hundreds of ways of preparing vegetables, and as they are such good value, it's worth looking at vegetables as something more than just a side dish. Roasting and chargrilling vegetables is very popular at the moment, and for good reason – if you've never roasted a pepper, try it today – the taste is sensational.

TABLES

HOW TO BOIL/BLANCH VEGETABLES

Boiling and blanching are the same thing really. Use a large pan, full of deep, boiling water. Vegetables take very little time to boil – the best way to check if they are cooked is to take one out, and eat it. They should always have a bit of crunch left. Make sure you drain them thoroughly.

To get maximum goodness from your vegetables, steam them rather than boiling. Steaming helps retain all the vitamins and minerals so plentiful in vegetables.

If you want to serve vegetables such as runner beans in a salad, boil them first, and then plunge them in a bowl of iced water to arrest the cooking. Don't just leave them to cool, as they will go soggy. Boiling vegetables rather than just serving them raw gives them a wonderful, intense colour (and makes them easier to chew).

You could use this method if you are preparing vegetables for a dinner party. Cook the vegetables in advance and plunge in iced water. When you are ready to serve them, simply plunge into boiling water for a few seconds to heat through again.

HOW TO CHARGRILL VEGETABLES

This is great way of cooking vegetables, and it draws out the most wonderful flavours. I suggest you invest in a griddle pan – it's possible to chargrill vegetables under a grill, but you'll find you have more control using a griddle pan. Cut your vegetables into large slices or wedges. Toss the vegetables in good olive oil, and place on a hot griddle pan. There is no need to boil the vegetables first. Slices of courgette, aubergine (dip the aubergine slices in flour first if you don't want them to absorb too much oil) and wedges of onion, fennel and peppers are all delicious chargrilled. When the vegetables start to colour, they are done, but as a rough guide, courgettes are the quickest, taking about 3 minutes, and fennel will take the longest, about 10 minutes. If you want to chargrill peppers, first remove the skins by roasting them in a hot oven for 2-3 minutes, until heated through and place in a polythene bag for 10 minutes. The steam will make removing the skins much easier. Rub some oil onto the skins and place on the griddle.

You can serve a selection of chargrilled vegetables as a salad, or use them as the filling for a really tasty vegetable lasagne.

Chargrilled VEGETABLE lasagne

To get the best flavours from the chargrilled vegetables, I marinate them overnight, so you need to start this recipe the day before you want to eat it.

serves 6

1 aubergine, sliced

2 courgettes, sliced

6 spring onions, blanched for 2 minutes

1 red pepper, roasted, skinned, deseeded and cut into four

1 yellow pepper, roasted, skinned, deseeded and cut into four

12 asparagus stalks, peeled if necessary

olive oil for dipping

1 shallot, peeled and diced

1 red chilli, deseeded and finely diced

1 clove garlic, peeled and diced

6 basil leaves, ripped

8 tablespoons olive oil

1 tablespoon sherry vinegar

600ml/1 pint cheese sauce

16 sheets lasagne

2 tablespoons grated Parmesan

2 tablespoons grated Gruyère

salt and freshly ground black pepper

1 Toss the aubergine, courgettes, spring onions, peppers and asparagus in olive oil and chargrill until cooked to your liking. You will need to do this in batches, as they won't all fit on together!

2 Mix together the shallot, chilli, garlic, basil leaves, 8 tablespoons of olive oil and the sherry vinegar to make a marinade.

3 Pour the marinade over the vegetables and mix together well. Leave overnight in the fridge.

4 To assemble the lasagne, place a layer of the vegetable mixture in the bottom of a large baking dish. Cover with sheets of lasagne, and then pour over some cheese sauce. Repeat until all the ingredients are used up, ending with a thick layer of cheese sauce.

5 Sprinkle with the grated Parmesan and Gruyère and bake in a preheated oven, gas mark 5/190°C/375°F for 45 minutes until the top is golden brown.

AUBERGINE curry

Serve this with warmed naan bread or plain, boiled rice.

serves 4

40 g/1½ oz tamarind pulp

½ cup hot water

500 g/1 lb aubergines

salt

2 teaspoons hot Indian-style curry paste

½ teaspoon mustard seeds

4 tablespoons olive oil

1 teaspoon freshly chopped ginger

1 garlic clove, chopped

8-10 curry leaves

2 onions, chopped

pinch of ground turmeric

125 g/4 oz desiccated coconut

2 cups cold water

juice of two limes

small bunch fresh coriander leaves

1 Soak the tamarind pulp in the hot water for 30 minutes.

2 Slash the aubergines deeply on each side, then soak in a large bowl of slightly salted water for 15 minutes. Drain, dry and cut into large pieces.

3 In a large, heavy-based frying pan, dry-roast the aubergines until golden, then add the curry paste. Stir well to coat the aubergine.

4 In a separate pan, sauté the mustard seeds in the olive oil for 1 minute.

5 Add the ginger, garlic and curry leaves, then sauté the ingredients for a few more minutes. Add the onion, turmeric and coconut. Cook until the onion has softened (about 4-5 minutes).

6 Add the cold water and dry-roasted aubergine, then add salt to taste.

7 Squeeze the soaked tamarind and push through a sieve resting over a bowl. Discard any residue left in the sieve, and pour the tamarind water into the aubergine mixture.

8 Cook the mixture until the aubergine becomes tender and the sauce has reduced. This should take about 20 minutes.

9 Sprinkle with the lime juice and coriander leaves to serve.

Root vegetables

Root vegetables (potatoes, onions, swedes, beetroot etc.) are the mainstay of the British diet. We can't get enough of them – we eat more spuds than almost anyone else. The Spanish, however, feed root vegetables to their cattle, but I guess it's just a matter of personal taste!

As British cooking has developed over the past few years, we've started to make better use of our root vegetables. Beetroot, for example, has terrified generations. But the day of the wobbly, pickled beetroot leaking all over your lettuce leaves is over. I suggest you pop a couple of beetroot in with your potatoes for a Sunday roast – the taste is sensational. Try mashed swede made with 65% swede and 35% butter, seasoned generously with freshly ground black pepper. You might as well be eating caviar – you will erase forever the memory of the watery swede you had at school.

I want to quash the myth that you have to cook all vegetables in boiling water. Root vegetables come from the cold earth, and you want to cook them starting with cold water. Bring the water to the boil with the vegetables in the pan. Leave the lid off, and don't add any salt – let the flavours of the vegetables speak for themselves.

CELERIAC

Celeriac doesn't make it onto our dining tables very often – I think the strange shape must put people off, but it's really easy to prepare. I suggest you try one of these recipes to ease you into it gently.

HOW TO COOK CELERIAC AND CARROT

Scrape a celeriac and a couple of carrots. Peeling root vegetables just wastes them. Chop the ends off the carrots. It's trendy to leave the green leaves on when boiling or steaming, and it does look quite good, but it doesn't actually add to the flavour. You will need to cut the root end of the celeriac off. Chop the celeriac and carrots into bite-sized pieces. I like to cut carrots into diagonal, thick slices, and if you can cut the celeriac into similar-sized pieces, that would be ideal. Put them in a large pan with enough cold water just to cover, 2 tablespoons of sugar and a knob of butter and bring to the boil.

Boil for about 15 minutes or until most of the liquid has evaporated, then place a circle of greaseproof paper on top, so it's just sitting on top of the water. When all the sugar has caramelised and coated the celeriac and carrot, remove from the pan. Sprinkle over some chopped dill and season with freshly ground black pepper.

CELERIAC AND APPLE PURÉE

This is a perfect accompaniment to game, roast pork and venison, or you could add stock to make a delicious soup. Scrape a celeriac and cut the root end off. Cut into bite-sized pieces. Peel and core a couple of cooking apples. You need about ⅔ the amount of apples to one whole celeriac. Chop the apples into large pieces. Place the celeriac in a large saucepan, add a bay leaf and cover with a half-and-half mixture of milk and water. Bring to the boil, and then add the apples. Cook for about 25 minutes. The apple will split the milk, but don't worry about that. When cooked, remove the bay leaf and drain the celeriac and apple mixture. Discard the liquid. Shake the celeriac and apple to remove any remaining liquid and then blend to a purée. Add a good dollop of cream and mix well.

HOW TO ROAST ROOT VEGETABLES

I suggest you try roasting any root vegetable you fancy – roasting really enhances the flavours of the vegetables, and they're robust enough to cope with the intense heat.

Cut beetroot into slivers because it takes ages to cook. Carrots, parsnips, leeks, swede, red onion and garlic are all fantastic roasted. Simply peel, cut into wedges, throw into a large roasting tray and drizzle with good olive oil. Chuck in plenty of thyme, rock salt and freshly ground black pepper and roast in a preheated oven at gas mark 5/190°C/375°F for 1-1½ hours. I suggest you take a peek after an hour to see how they are getting on. When cooked, remove from the oven and toss in balsamic vinegar while still warm, and serve.

ROOT VEGETABLE
gratin dauphinoise

This gratin can quite happily stand on its own as a tasty and substantial main course (serving 4 people). Alternatively, it works just as well as an accompaniment to a meat main dish (serving 6-8 people).

serves 4

4 medium carrots, thinly sliced
50 g/2 oz butter
2 cloves garlic, finely chopped
200 g/7 oz Emmenthal, grated
3 medium potatoes, thinly sliced
1 small swede, sliced
2 small parsnips, sliced
300 ml/½ pint milk
300 ml/½ pint cream
1 medium egg, beaten
3 tablespoons breadcrumbs

1 Place the carrots in the bottom of a medium-sized baking dish. Add the butter and a pinch of the garlic.

2 Sprinkle over some of the grated Emmenthal.

3 Layer the swede over, and add a couple more knobs of butter, and a little more garlic. Repeat with the parsnips, and finally the potato.

4 Sprinkle over the remaining cheese.

5 Mix together the milk, cream and egg, and pour evenly over the vegetables.

6 Top with the breadcrumbs and bake the gratin in a preheated oven at gas mark 5/190°C/375°F for 45 minutes.

BORSCHT

This is a very simple,
cold borscht.

serves 4

4 large cooked beetroot, cut
into chunks

1 tablespoon olive oil

2 large white onions, very
finely chopped

2 sticks celery, very finely chopped

1 tablespoon good red wine or
sherry vinegar

2 tablespoons freshly
chopped parsley

salt and freshly ground
black pepper

200 ml/7 fl oz cream

1 Blend the beetroot in a blender to a rough purée. Add water gradually until you get the consistency of a thick soup. If you have cooked the beetroot yourself, use the cooking liquid. Don't aim for a super-smooth purée; a bit of texture is much better.

2 Heat the oil in a medium saucepan, and sauté the onion and celery until well softened, for about 10 minutes.

3 Drain off the oil and add the onion to the beetroot mixture.

4 Stir in the red wine or sherry vinegar and parsley and season to taste.

5 Lastly, whisk in the cream. Serve chilled.

Potatoes

The Brits have always been dedicated fans of spuds, and we consume a vast amount — baked, roasted, boiled, mashed or however else we can think of to eat them. Although they have a high carbohydrate content, we shouldn't think of potatoes as unhealthy vegetables. In fact, baked potatoes are low in fat, and with their roughage-giving skins (I hope you're not one of those who scrapes the potato out and leaves the skin!) are nutritious and full of goodness. So as long as you don't pile on the butter or mayonnaise, then there's no need to feel too bad about eating plenty of spuds.

Old potatoes are available from September to June, in this country. They are the ones to use for baking, mashing, and for making chips. This is because they contain lots of starch. The ones I'd recommend are King Edward, Maris Piper, Cara and Desiree.

New potatoes appear from early May. They are waxier than old potatoes, and are ideal for boiling. The best ones, without a doubt, are Jersey potatoes.

HOW TO BOIL OR STEAM POTATOES

Boiling brings out the natural flavour of vegetables, and it is the best way to cook new potatoes. If you buy a good variety, you really don't need to do anything more than boil or steam, then serve with plenty of butter.

It is important to cook potatoes so that they are cooked evenly throughout. For best results, simmer them slowly. Place your potatoes (whole, if new; cut into large pieces, if old) in a pan. Cover with cold water and bring to the boil. Simmer for 12-20 minutes, depending on the type of potato. To check if they are cooked, stick a knife into the centre of a potato. If cooked, it will meet with no resistance.

Steaming potatoes retains the nutrients. You could use a metal or wooden steamer that fits over a large saucepan, or you could use a metal sieve. They all work in the same way. The water in the saucepan should be simmering gently. Place your steamer containing the vegetables over the top, and steam for about 12 minutes.

HOW TO MAKE PERFECT CHIPS

The secret of perfect chips lies in the temperature, so you really need a temperature-controlled deep-fat fryer for the purpose. You should blanch them in boiling water for 2-3 minutes, and then dry with kitchen paper. Fry them first at gas mark 3/160°C/325°F for 5-6 minutes. This will cook the chips. Then put the fryer up to gas mark 5/190°C/375°F for a further 3 minutes to crisp them up. Shake well, and serve sprinkled with plenty of salt.

HOW TO MAKE MASHED POTATOES

THE FRENCH WAY...

The French call their mashed potato 'pomme purée', and it is very different to our beloved mash. Boil the potatoes, and then drain them well in a colander. Place over a low heat to dry them. Force the potatoes through a mouli or ricer, and then whizz in a blender with plenty of good quality olive oil to make a purée. It should be so runny that it pours!

THE ENGLISH WAY...

Use large, floury potatoes such as King Edward's, and boil until cooked. Drain, and then place over a low heat to dry them. Using a traditional potato masher, mash with milk and /or cream until you get to the consistency you like. You could add a pinch of nutmeg or some butter, if you like. To serve, make a well in the potato, and add a large lump of butter. If you have any leftover mashed potato, use it for Bubble and Squeak (see page 82).

HOW TO BAKE POTATOES

Use large, floury potatoes such as King Edward's. Scrub well, and then push a metal skewer all the way through the potatoes. I don't know why people like to wrap potatoes in foil, because that just steams them, and they don't get that lovely, crispy skin. So, forget the foil. Place the potatoes on a baking sheet, on a bed of rock salt and bake in a preheated oven at gas mark 7/220°C/425°F for 1 hour. If you don't use skewers, they can take up to 2 hours. Try these with truffled eggs (see page 83).

HOW TO ROAST POTATOES

Use large, floury potatoes such as King Edward's. As you have probably found out, new potatoes and other waxy potatoes don't produce the fluffy, crisp, roast potatoes that we all love. Roasted new potatoes are very nice – but very different. Cut your potatoes into large pieces and boil them in salted water for 10 minutes, or until they start flaking. Drain them well by giving them a good shake in a colander. It's good if they get a bit bashed up because this gives them rough edges which will crisp up nicely. Sprinkle them with flour and then place in a large roasting dish containing piping hot dripping or lard. I like to throw in a few cloves of garlic and some bay leaves to heat up with the oil – it all adds to the flavour. Make sure the potatoes are covered with fat, then roast for ½ hour at gas mark 6/200°C/400°F. Drain the fat and then continue to roast for a further 10 minutes to crisp them up.

BUBBLE & SQUEAK

with poached eggs & hollandaise sauce

This is a substantial
brunch dish.

serves 2

125 g/4 oz butter

1 onion, chopped

½ teaspoon chopped thyme

4 rashers bacon

125 g/4 oz cabbage

125 g/4 oz mashed potato

1 teaspoon dripping

4 medium eggs

6 peppercorns

3 tablespoons lemon juice or
white wine vinegar

2 egg yolks

salt and freshly ground
black pepper

1 Melt half the butter in a
large frying pan, and fry
the onion and thyme until the
onion softens. Meanwhile, grill
the bacon rashers.

2 In a bowl, mix together
the onion mixture,
cabbage and mashed potato.
Season with salt and freshly
ground black pepper.

3 Melt the dripping in a
frying pan and add the
potato mix. Push it down to
make an omelette shape. When
it goes crispy around the sides,
turn it over and cook until both
sides are golden and crispy.

4 Next, poach the eggs.
Bring a large saucepan
of water to the boil, and break
each egg into a small cup or
bowl. Carefully drop the eggs
into the water and cook for
2-3 minutes. Remove the eggs
and plunge into cold water.

5 Put the peppercorns,
lemon juice or white
wine vinegar in a clean frying
pan and heat until the liquid is
reduced a little. Meanwhile,
melt the remaining butter in a
separate pan.

6 Strain the lemon juice
mixture to remove the
peppercorns, add the two egg
yolks and whisk together.
Slowly add the melted butter a
little at a time, whisking the
mixture constantly. When you

Baked
POTATO
with truffled eggs

serves 2

2 baked potatoes
25 g/1 oz butter
3 teaspoons truffle paste
4 tablespoons crème fraîche
4 tablespoons double cream
2 medium eggs
salt and freshly ground
black pepper

have added all the butter, place the bowl over a pan of boiling water and continue to whisk until the sauce is thick and creamy. This is a 'hollandaise' sauce. Taste the sauce, and add a little salt if necessary.

7 Cut the bubble and squeak in half (or use a round pastry cutter if you want to be neat) and place on two plates. Re-heat the poached eggs in boiling water and place on top of the bubble and squeak. Pour over the hollandaise sauce and cover with the bacon rashers.

1 Slice off the top third of the two baked potatoes. Using a dessertspoon, scoop out the inside of the potatoes, leaving a little around the edges.

2 Place the potato in a bowl and mash roughly with the butter. Season to taste with salt and freshly ground black pepper.

3 In a separate bowl, mix together the truffle paste, crème fraîche and the double cream.

4 Divide half the truffle mixture between the baked potatoes, and then break an egg into each potato. Carefully spoon the rest of the truffle paste over the raw egg and then fill the potato with the mashed potato mixture.

5 Place the potatoes under a hot grill until they turn golden brown.

PULSES

We used only to be able to buy butter beans and split peas, but with the growing trend towards vegetarianism, we have been introduced to all kinds of wonderful beans and pulses. The introduction of Indian and Middle Eastern foods into our diets has further developed this trend, and we are seeing lentils and all manner of beans in restaurants and supermarkets. And rightly so, because beans and pulses are rich in minerals, vitamins and fibre, yet are very low in fat, and very inexpensive, and don't forget – they taste great. If you haven't tried cooking with beans and pulses, you really should have a go at one of these recipes – you'll wonder what took you so long.

Dried beans are very cheap, and well worth buying, but you need to soak them before cooking. You could buy beans sold in cans, as they have already been soaked, but you will pay a fair bit more for them.

Choose from aduki beans, black and black-eye beans, cannellini beans, mung beans, pinto beans and the familiar red kidney beans, to name but a few. I've used flageolet beans in the lamb recipe on page 60.

Lentils are all the rage at the moment, appearing on restaurant menus everywhere you look. They are also a key ingredient in Middle Eastern and Indian cookery, especially in dishes such as dahl. Confusingly perhaps, dahl is the Indian name for lentil. You don't need to soak lentils before cooking. Red lentils take just 20 minutes to cook, and brown, yellow and puy lentils, 30-40 minutes. Simply cover with water and simmer gently.

HOW TO SOAK BEANS

Cover your beans with cold water so the water level is 10 cm/4 in above the beans. Soak overnight, and then rinse well. Boil

& BEANS

them in fresh water before you start cooking. This will destroy any harmful toxins.

HOW TO MAKE DAHL

Place your red lentils in a large saucepan and add enough water to just cover. Bring to the boil and simmer until the lentils are very soft (about 30-40 minutes). Add more water if necessary during the cooking time. Melt some ghee or butter in a large frying pan and gently fry some chopped garlic and ginger until soft. Add cayenne pepper, turmeric, cumin seeds and lemon juice and heat through until bubbling. Add the lentils and cook for a further 5 minutes. Add some chopped coriander and baby spinach leaves, and stir well. When the leaves have wilted, serve with wedges of lime. You could water the dahl down to make a tasty lentil soup.

HOW TO MAKE BAKED BEANS

If you ever decide to become a cowboy, this is the recipe for authentic, American baked beans. It takes about 4 hours to make, but tastes a hundred times better than tinned baked beans. Cook some kidney beans in simmering water for about 1 hour. Meanwhile, melt some olive oil in a large saucepan and gently fry some chopped onion, peppers, garlic, carrot and bacon until the carrot is soft. Add a bay leaf, some thyme and crushed coriander seeds, and cook for a further 10 minutes. Add 1 tablespoon of tomato purée and a tin of chopped tomatoes. When cooked, drain the kidney beans and add to the tomato mixture. Transfer to a large casserole dish and cover with water. Bake in a preheated oven at gas mark 3/160°C/325°F for 1½-2 hours until the beans have soaked up all the juices. Stir in a few tablespoons of maple syrup and serve.

PUY LENTILS

with bacon & mushrooms

Cèpes (called porcini in Italy) are delicious wild mushrooms. They impart the most wonderful flavour, and as you can get them in almost every supermarket these days, don't be tempted to substitute any other kind of mushroom.

serves 4

1 tablespoon olive oil

50 g/2 oz smoky bacon, cut into pieces

2 onions, finely diced

2 sprigs thyme

2 sticks celery, finely diced

2 carrots, finely diced

3 cloves garlic, crushed

50 g/2 oz dried cèpes/porcini mushrooms, soaked in hot water for ½ hour

1 bottle red wine

500 g/1 lb puy lentils

600 ml/1 pint chicken stock

1 Heat the olive oil in a large saucepan, then add the bacon and onion. Cook until the onion is soft but not brown.

2 Add the thyme, celery, carrots and garlic and fry gently for 5-8 minutes.

3 Meanwhile squeeze the cèpes in your hand, until all the water has been squeezed out, and reserve the liquid. Chop them finely and add to the pan.

4 Add ⅓ of the red wine and the liquid from the cèpes. Do this carefully as there will be grit in the bottom of the bowl, from the cèpes. Try not to let this pour into the pan. Add the lentils, the rest of the wine and the stock. Bring to the boil and then simmer for 1 hour. The lentils should be soft and should have absorbed most of the liquid.

PISTOU SOUP

Pistou is the French version of Italy's pesto, and it is also the name given to this French soup. If you like the flavour, you could make extra pistou to mix with pasta, to give it an interesting kick.

serves 4-6

3 cloves garlic

pinch of rock salt

1 bunch basil leaves

olive oil

1 onion, finely chopped

200 g/7 oz tinned, chopped tomatoes

2 potatoes, diced

2 carrots, sliced

2 leeks, sliced

600 ml/1 pint vegetable stock

1 tin of haricot beans, drained and rinsed

1 courgette, diced

50 g/2 oz French beans

handful of spinach leaves (optional)

1 To make pistou, crush 2 cloves of garlic and the salt in a pestle and mortar. Add the basil leaves and crush them to a pulp. Dribble a little olive oil in the mortar and grind into a paste. Add more oil if necessary.

2 Chop the remaining clove of garlic. Heat 1 tablespoon of olive oil in a large frying pan and add the onion and chopped garlic. Cook until the onion is soft, but not brown. Add the tomatoes and cook on a high heat for 2 minutes.

3 Add the potatoes, carrots, leeks and stock and simmer for 15 minutes.

4 Add the haricot beans, courgette, French beans and spinach, if using. Cook gently for about 2 minutes, or until the spinach has wilted. Serve the soup with the pistou spooned on top.

SALAD

In this chapter I'm looking at salad dressing, and how to make three classic salads. The shops are filled with ready-made salads and dressings, but when you see how simple it is to make the ones I'm showing you here, I hope you won't resort to them. I'm quite a fan of the bags of lettuce you can buy — they are coming down in price, and are very useful for one or two people, on those occasions when it would be wasteful to buy two or three kinds of lettuce, only to throw away half of it. Bottled salad dressing can be a waste of time and money too. Only the expensive ones have decent ingredients (without loads of additives), and even with additives they don't last for very long. It's a much better idea to make up a little amount of salad dressing to use as and when you need it. It's more fun too.

We are spoilt for choice for salad leaves at the moment. We all have our own favourites, but don't be scared to try some new varieties. English butter lettuce and iceberg are excellent for many salads, and nothing beats iceberg for adding crunch to a burger, but for variety and flavour try frisée (curly endive), radicchio and chicory (the leaf tips should be yellow not green). Fresh herbs add welcome zip to a salad, so don't be afraid to throw a few in. To avoid soggy salads, buy a plastic salad spinner. They cost practically nothing, and they are invaluable for draining and drying your salad. If you like to add tomatoes and cucumbers etc. to salad, try to be a little different and have a good look around the supermarket for new ideas. Almost anything goes. One word though about tomatoes: unfortunately, plum tomatoes seem to be the only variety that have any flavour at the moment, so try to buy these.

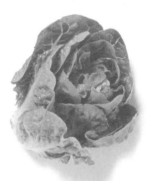

HOW TO MAKE A BASIC SALAD DRESSING

This is so easy! Measure out 4 parts of oil to 1 part vinegar. For one or two people, this is literally 4 tablespoons oil to 1 tablespoon vinegar. Choose a good oil (extra virgin olive oil is the best) and a good vinegar (red wine vinegar, or balsamic for a fabulous flavour). Add a pinch of salt and freshly ground black pepper and shake or whisk until mixed. That's it!

To make a vinaigrette, add 1 teaspoon of Dijon mustard, and if you fancy, a pinch of fresh herbs or chopped garlic; tarragon is one of my favourites. Shake or whisk well.

You can keep these in the fridge for ages, but I suggest that you remove the dressings from the fridge an hour or so before you want to use, so the dressing is at room temperature. Always give it another shake before serving.

For a light lunch, add some crispy bacon and croutons to a basic vinaigrette and pour over a tasty selection of salad leaves.

HOW TO MAKE MAYONNAISE

Once you've tried real mayonnaise, you'll never want to buy one of those large jars again. You'll need a strong wrist or a food processor for this. Beat together 2 egg yolks, 1 teaspoon of English mustard, a squeeze of lemon juice and salt and freshly ground black pepper. Beat well, then add 350 ml/12 fl oz of olive oil very slowly, beating continually. If the mixture starts to split, add a drop of warm water. Beat until it starts to turn white.

HOW TO MAKE BLUE CHEESE DRESSING

Use about 300 ml/½ pint of mayonnaise for the base. Add 3 tablespoons of soured cream, a few chopped spring onions, 1 stalk of celery (finely chopped), a mashed clove of garlic and then mash in 75 g/3 oz of blue cheese. The ingredients should be mixed, but not to a purée – a real treat on jacket potatoes.

SALAD niçoise

Caesar SALAD

'Niçoise' is a French phrase that means 'as prepared in Nice', but it is a dish that has travelled all over the world. This salad is packed full of good things – you feel virtuous just looking at it. A bag of selected soft salad leaves is ideal for this recipe.

Said to have been created in the 20s by an Italian chef, Caesar Cardini, who lived in Mexico. Purists would use romaine lettuce, but it's tricky to find here.

serves 2

2 tablespoons olive oil

1 teaspoon white wine vinegar

200 g/7 oz French beans, freshly boiled

2 ripe tomatoes, cut into wedges

200 g/7 oz can tuna chunks in olive oil, drained

2 hard-boiled eggs, quartered

2-4 potatoes, freshly boiled, cut into bite-size chunks

2 large handfuls of soft salad leaves

16 small black olives

8 anchovies, split lengthwise

salt and freshly ground black pepper

1 Beat together the olive oil, vinegar and salt and pepper to make a basic salad dressing.

2 Gently mix together the beans, tomato, tuna, egg and potato, then pour over the dressing. Mix carefully.

3 Divide the salad leaves between two salad bowls or plates and divide the bean mixture between the two.

4 Scatter over the olives, and place the anchovies on top.

serves 2

2 egg yolks

1 clove garlic

2 anchovies

2 teaspoon Dijon mustard

1½ fl oz white wine vinegar

1 teaspoon Worcester sauce

100 ml/3½ fl oz olive oil and 1 tablespoon for frying

100 ml/3½ fl oz vegetable oil

1 cos lettuce, cut into bite-size pieces

125 g/¼ lb fresh Parmesan, grated

4 slices of baguette, cut into croutons

Tagliatelle with butter & ROCKET

Be warned – this salad has so much butter in it, it's in the name! Certainly not a salad for dieters. Rocket is also known as arugula or rucola.

serves 2

2 handfuls of rocket leaves
3 spring onions, sliced
175 g/6 oz unsalted butter
500 g/1 lb fresh tagliatelle
6 basil leaves, ripped
16 black olives, stoned
freshly grated Parmesan, to serve
salt and freshly ground
black pepper

1 Start by making the dressing. Place the egg yolks into a blender with the garlic, anchovies, Dijon mustard, white wine vinegar and the Worcester sauce. Whizz until blended.

2 Meanwhile, in a pouring jug, mix the olive oil with the vegetable oil. With the blender on a slow setting, slowly pour the oil mixture into the blender. If the dressing looks like splitting, add 1 teaspoon of water.

3 Heat the remaining olive oil in a small frying pan, and fry the croutons until nice and crispy.

4 Mix the lettuce and Parmesan with the dressing and serve sprinkled with the croutons.

1 Tear the rocket leaves into rough pieces, removing any tough stems, then place in a large salad bowl with the spring onions.

2 In a small frying pan, melt the butter and pour over the rocket leaves.

3 Meanwhile, in a large saucepan of boiling water, cook the pasta for 2-3 minutes until *al dente* (with a little 'bite').

4 Drain the pasta and pour onto the rocket and butter. The heat of the pasta will cook and wilt the rocket leaves. Fold in the basil and black olives, season to taste and serve liberally sprinkled with Parmesan.

CHILLIES

Did you know that there are over 150 varieties of chilli available in the United States (where it is spelt 'chili' or 'chile')? Britain is a little way behind that, but we are slowly catching up. Chillies are a vital ingredient in all manner of cuisines, from Mexican to Indian, and as these cuisines are so popular, I thought it was worth telling you a few things about them. The hottest chilli is Scotch Bonnet, which looks like a mini red pepper. It's so strong that if you put it in your mouth for just a few seconds, you would be chasing your tail for miles. It's a sneaky one, because generally, the larger the chilli, the milder it is – but not in this case!

Whole chillies are widely available these days, but we have had chillies for a long time in the herbs and spices section at the supermarket. Did you realise that cayenne and paprika are chillies? Most of us are familiar with chilli powder, and you can also buy chilli paste. Chinese cookery tends to use chilli paste and in London's Chinatown, you would be able to find about 40 different types of chilli paste. Chilli is also the main ingredient in Tabasco sauce. Chillies vary in hotness, from moderate jalapeño chillies to the hot bird's eye chillies often used in Thai cookery. Most of a chilli's heat is centred in its seeds and membrane, so removing those

will make even the hottest chilli a little more tolerable – but where's the fun in that?

HOW TO HANDLE CHILLIES

Chillies are truly wicked things – be careful how you handle them because if you touch any sensitive areas of your body after handling them, it will hurt. Wear rubber gloves while handling, or if you find this makes you clumsy, rub your hands with olive oil. This clogs your pores, so the chilli can't affect you. Prepare chillies by slicing down the side of the chilli, and scraping out the seeds and membrane. The chillies are now ready for use in a recipe.

HOW TO MAKE CHILLI SAUCE

You can serve this with all sorts of things, but it is great with grilled meat. Heat a little olive oil in a large saucepan and add some chopped onion, chilli flakes, garlic, dried chillies, 1 teaspoon cumin and a splash of sherry vinegar. As the chillies hit the heat, your eyes will start to stream. Add a tin of chopped tomatoes and season with salt and freshly ground black pepper. Cook over a gentle heat until the onion is soft and the sauce is reduced. Purée if you want a smooth chilli sauce, or leave chunky.

HOW TO MAKE TOMATO SALSA

For us 'salsa' is the word for a spicy Mexican chopped dip, but for the Mexicans it is simply the word for sauce – which says a lot about how they like their cooking! I'm sure they use it for all their sauces, not just the hot and spicy ones. We tend to think of sauces as cooked, whereas salsa is raw.

Mix together some finely chopped tomatoes, red onion, a green and red chilli, garlic and coriander. Add a large splash of lime juice, and about 4 times as much olive oil as lime juice. Season with salt and pepper and leave for ½ hour before serving to let the flavours develop. Serve with grilled fish and meat.

You could also do this recipe with red and yellow peppers, instead of the tomatoes.

HOW TO STUFF CHILLIES

If you want a little canapé to wake up your guests, try these stuffed chillies. Try to buy a jar of Scotch Bonnet chillies (they come bottled in brine). Mash together a small log of goat's cheese, a chopped shallot and garlic clove, some chopped fresh herbs and season with salt and freshly ground black pepper. Using a teaspoon or piping bag, fill the chillies with the cheese mixture. Bake or grill at a medium heat for 6-7 minutes, or until the cheese bubbles. Serve warm, if possible.

HOW TO MAKE FRESH CORN SALSA

Barbecue or grill a couple of corn-on-the-cobs, then break off the kernels. Prepare a chilli or two as explained earlier, and chop finely. Then mix the chilli and corn together and add a pinch of marjoram or oregano, a few chopped sun-dried tomatoes, a splash of lime juice, and about 4 times as much olive oil as lime juice. Season with salt and pepper and mix well.

Green chicken CURRY

Once you've tried this, you won't want to use one of those ready-made sauces again.

serves 4

4 cups coconut milk

2 tablespoons green curry paste

600 ml/1 pint chicken stock

1.25 kg/3 lb boneless chicken thighs

small handful of citrus (kaffir) leaves

2 tablespoons fish sauce

2 tablespoons finely chopped chillies, seeds removed

4 tablespoons finely chopped fresh basil or coriander leaves

1 Heat a wok or large frying pan, and add half the coconut milk. Bring to the boil and simmer gently for 4-5 minutes until the milk reduces.

2 Add the curry paste and stir into the milk. Add the stock and stir until the coconut milk splits.

3 Add the chicken thighs and stir well. Bring to the boil, and simmer for 15 minutes until the chicken is cooked.

4 Add the citrus leaves, chillies, fish sauce and the remainder of the coconut milk. Cook for another 15-20 minutes, until the sauce is reduced by half.

5 Just before serving, add half the basil or coriander leaves and stir. To serve, lift the chicken from the wok or frying pan, and place on a plate or serving dish. Pour the sauce over and garnish with the remaining basil or coriander.

Grilled Yucatán
CHILLI prawns with papaya

I have suggested you use a medium-strength chilli for this recipe, but you could use a different strength chilli, according to your taste. To crumble the oregano, simply rub in your hands – this releases the wonderful flavour. This is good served with one of the salsas previously mentioned.

serves 2

1 orange

2 limes

3 cloves garlic, chopped

1 medium-hot green or red chilli, chopped

2 tablespoons mild chilli powder

2 teaspoons paprika

1 teaspoon cumin

½ teaspoon crumbled oregano

½ teaspoon salt

2 tablespoons olive oil

500 g/1 lb large prawns, unshelled

1 firm but ripe papaya, peeled and cut into bite-size pieces

1 Grate the rind of the orange and one of the limes, then squeeze the juice. Combine the juice and grated rind with the garlic, chilli, chilli powder, paprika, cumin, oregano, salt and olive oil.

2 Add the prawns and stir well so all the prawns are coated. Leave to marinate for 1 hour.

3 Thread the prawns onto a skewer, then grill over a charcoal fire if possible, otherwise a normal grill, for 3-4 minutes or until cooked.

4 Thread on the papaya and wedges of lime and serve immediately.

Opposite
Right: Panzanella (page 108), *Left*: White Chocolate Bread and Butter Pudding (page 109).

Overleaf
Summer Pudding (page 99).

FRUIT
Summer fruits

Summer fruits are basically soft fruits such as strawberries, raspberries, peaches and apricots, to name but a few. Unfortunately, the name 'summer' no longer really applies, as we can buy these fruits almost all year round. However, if you want to buy fruit at its very best, stick to the seasons, and try to buy British soft fruits in the summer. Not only are they cheapest at this time of the year; the flavour is also at its best.

HOW TO MAKE A RASPBERRY COULIS

This is a very simple fruit sauce, which is delicious served with all manner of desserts and ice creams. Simply whizz raspberries (you could try any kind of soft fruit) in a food processor, with icing sugar and lime juice. You will only need a small handful of raspberries per person; a punnet will probably be enough for about 6 people. For a whole punnet, you will need to add 2 teaspoons of sugar, and the juice of 1 lime. Fresh raspberries will give the best flavour, but frozen raspberries aren't bad. Sieve the purée, and discard the seeds. The coulis should be quite runny, so add a little cold water if necessary. Serve drizzled around a slice of dessert or over ice cream.

HOW TO MAKE RASPBERRY SORBET

Using about 50 g/2 oz of caster sugar and an equal measure of water, melt together the sugar and water in a saucepan to make a syrup. Add a bay leaf and a little grated orange peel, and stir until the sugar has melted. Sieve, to remove the bay leaf and orange peel, and stir the syrup into a raspberry coulis, made as above, from 1 punnet of raspberries. Pour into an ice cream machine, and churn for about ½ hour. I don't like to add egg whites, as I think it makes the sorbet cloudy. When ready, serve with a sprig of mint, and a fresh raspberry.

BLUEBERRY muffins

You could use chocolate chips or raspberries in place of the blueberries.

**makes
12 muffins**

4 tablespoons vegetable oil, plus extra for greasing

200 g/7 oz plain flour

2 teaspoons baking powder

125 g/4 oz sugar

¾ cup milk or buttermilk

1 medium egg

200 g/7 oz blueberries, halved

1 Thoroughly grease a 12-hole muffin tray with vegetable oil. This is best done in advance, so the batter doesn't have to wait before being poured into the tray.

2 Sift the flour and baking powder together into a large mixing bowl, and gently stir in the sugar.

3 In a separate bowl, mix the milk or buttermilk, egg and the 4 tablespoons of oil together. Make a well in the centre of flour and slowly fold in the liquid. When all the liquid is added, beat well, and add the blueberries.

4 Spoon the mixture into the prepared muffin tray until each cup is about ⅔ full. Bake in a preheated oven at gas mark 4/180°C/350°F for 20-25 minutes. You can test whether the muffins are cooked by lightly pressing one; if the top springs back, they are ready.

5 Cool the muffins on a wire rack. You can eat them on their own, but I think they are best when served slightly warm, split, and spread with butter and jam.

SUMMER pudding

This is such a classic – if you've never made one before, please have a go – it's easy, virtually fat free (though I think it's best served with double cream!), and tastes delicious.

serves 6–8

350 g/11½ oz selection of mixed berries, such as blackcurrants, redcurrants and raspberries

3 tablespoons orange juice

100 g/3½ oz caster sugar

3 tablespoons water

450 g/15 oz strawberries, hulled and quartered

10 slices medium-sliced white bread, crusts removed

mint sprigs, to decorate

1 Place the mixed berries in a large saucepan with the orange juice, sugar and water. Simmer gently for 5 minutes, and then add the strawberries. Stir well, then remove from the heat, and leave to stand for 5 minutes.

2 Drain the fruit and put the liquid to one side. From one of the slices of bread, cut out a circle large enough to fit the base of a 1.2 litre/2 pint basin. Cut the remaining slices of bread in half.

3 Dip all the bread in the fruit liquid, then line the basin with the slices of bread, starting with the circle, and reserving 5 slices for the top. Make sure you overlap the pieces around the sides.

4 Spoon the fruit into the basin, pressing down well. Top with the remaining pieces of bread and spoon the fruit liquid over, reserving about 4 tablespoons.

5 Cover the pudding with a saucer and weight it down with something quite heavy – you could use two or three full tin cans. Leave in the fridge overnight.

6 To serve, turn out the pudding onto a plate. Spoon the reserved syrup over the top and decorate with a few mint sprigs.

Baked amaretti
PEACHES

This is extremely alcoholic, so make sure you don't have to drive anywhere after eating one of these peaches.

serves 3

3 peaches
175 g/6 oz unsalted butter, plus extra for greasing
20-25 amaretti biscuits
½ bottle Amaretto liqueur

1 Slice the peaches in half and remove all the stones. Place them in a well-buttered dish.

2 In a blender, whisk together the amaretti biscuits, butter and a splash of Amaretto liqueur. When fairly smooth, spoon the mixture into the centre of each peach.

3 Pour the rest of the Amaretto liquor over the peaches and bake them in an oven for 20-45 minutes, depending on the hardness of the peaches. If the peaches are very soft, cook for just 20 minutes. They should be very soft when done.

Tropical

Although I am not particularly happy about imported summer fruits (because we can do the job ourselves), I am delighted about imported tropical fruits. There are some wonderful fruits out there, and they make great desserts served simply on their own. I like to eat tropical fruits for breakfast – they make a zingy start to the day. As some of the tropical fruits are still quite new to us, I thought I'd take you through what to look out for, and how to eat some of the trickier ones! Thankfully, they are well-labelled in the shops, so I don't need to describe to you what they look like.

fruits

PINEAPPLE to know which one to choose, have a smell. If it smells sweet, then it will be sweet to eat. Also, choose one that doesn't have green bits on the skin spikes. To prepare a pineapple, cut the bottom off, so you can sit the pineapple. You can cut the top off, or leave it on; it might be good to leave it on, to give you something to hold onto. Slice the skin off downwards, using a good, sharp knife. Cut out the diagonal tramlines to get rid of the brown circles. This might sound strange, but when you look at a pineapple, it will become clear.

KEYWANU this looks great, but unfortunately doesn't taste of anything, so save your money.

BANANAS we all know a fair bit about bananas, but did you know you should never store them in a fridge? They will go black overnight.

KIWIS the kiwi got such abuse in the 80s, and I think it should be put back on the map. Kiwis are absolutely delicious, easy to eat, and look great – so Save The Kiwi Fruit! To eat, simply cut the top off, and eat with a teaspoon, as you would a boiled egg. Otherwise, peel using a small, sharp knife, and slice.

GRENADILLO this is worth trying. They taste a bit like lychees, so if you are a fan, try a few served with vanilla ice cream.

TAMARILLO this is also known as tree tomato. You can't really eat this raw, but it's excellent cooked gently, as you would for plums. I particularly like them in compotes.

PHYSALIS also known as Chinese lanterns, Chinese gooseberries or strawberry tomatoes. These are the bright orange cherry-size fruits that come wrapped in pale, golden leaves. They are often used as decoration, but they also taste very good.

STAR FRUIT *for me, the only value these have is for decoration – tastewise, they are a complete waste of space.*

MANGO *eating these won't be new to most people, but preparing them can be a little tricky. A mango has a wide and a narrow side. Cut along the narrow side ridge, and carefully cut around the flat stone, to create 2 halves. Score the flesh of the 2 halves, to make a small, criss-cross pattern, then turn inside out. You could then eat this, or cut off the chunks to use for chutney.*

MANGOSHIRE *This is not at all like a mango; it looks more like a lychee. Insert a knife, and cut all around the stone in the middle. Pull apart, then eat the insides with a teaspoon.*

RAMBUTAN *this has a distinctive red colour and is gradually becoming more available. Slice all around, pull apart and eat the middle, with a teaspoon.*

PASSION FRUIT *these are ripe and ready to eat when they look mottled and bumpy. This seems to put people off and supermarkets actually reduce them when they start to look like this! Slice in half, and eat with a teaspoon. Passion fruit are delicious in sorbets.*

LYCHEES *peel with your fingers, and nibble around the stone, as if eating a cherry.*

PAWPAW *this is also known as papaya. Treat like a melon; cut into large wedges, and scrape out the seeds. I like pawpaw sprinkled with lime juice; you don't need to add sugar.*

FRUIT KEBABS

This is so easy, and is a great dessert for barbecues. You can use any selection of tropical fruit that you like – I find mango, banana, pawpaw and pineapple work well. Simply peel all the fruit and cut it into bite-size chunks. Feed the chunks onto skewers (if you are using wooden skewers, soak them in water first). To make a glaze, mix together some rum, lime juice and melted butter and baste this over the kebabs when barbecuing. You could cook these in a frying pan or griddle pan. It will only take about 6-7 minutes to cook the kebabs; they are done when the fruit starts to go brown. Heat any remaining glaze to reduce it a little, and serve the kebabs with a little more sauce poured over, and a wedge of lime.

Duck salad with MANGO salsa

A lovely, light way to serve duck.

1 large breast duck
1 mango, diced
1 small bunch mint, chopped
1 small bunch coriander, chopped
juice of 1 lime
1 red onion, diced
1 chilli, finely chopped
3 tomatoes, diced
dash of olive oil
salt and freshly ground
black pepper

serves 4

1 To prepare the duck score criss-crosses on its skin; this allows some of the fat to be released when cooking.

2 Place the duck skin-side down in a medium frying pan over a medium heat and cook for 4-5 minutes. Turn over, and cook for a further 2-3 minutes. Place the frying pan straight into a preheated oven at gas mark 5/190°C/375°F for a further 2-3 minutes.

3 Meanwhile, to make the salsa, combine the remaining ingredients, season well, and add a good dash of olive oil.

4 When the duck is cooked it will feel firm. Remove from the oven and slice into 1 cm/½ in pieces. Serve with the mango salsa.

Tropical FRUIT smoothie

150 ml/¼ pint orange juice
a few cubes of ice
6 strawberries, halved and hulled
1 papaya, thinly sliced
1 teaspoon honey
300 ml/½ pint Greek yoghurt
2 tablespoons wheatgerm
1 mango, diced
1 banana, sliced

serves 1

1 Pour the orange juice into a blender with some ice, and whizz for about 20 seconds. Add the strawberries and papaya and whizz for a further 20 seconds.

2 Add the honey, yoghurt, wheatgerm and blend for 20 seconds. Add the mango, whizz for 20 seconds, add the banana, and then whizz for a further 20 seconds. By blending in stages, you ensure your smoothie is truly smooth. Serve immediately in a tall glass.

Orchard fruits

By orchard fruits I mean apples, pears and plums – all good, classic, British fare. Would you believe that there are over 150 varieties of apple? And yet we only ever see 5 or 6 varieties in the shops. I'm not a great fan of French apples, because I find them a bit bland and woolly. You just can't beat British Bramley and Cox's apples for cooking. In our quest for perfect, unblemished fruit, we've encouraged breeders to breed out all the flavour from our apples, and the supermarkets just stock those apples that look the best – irrespective of flavour. The same is happening with pears, though Conference and Comice pears aren't bad. The best plum is Victoria. Look for them in a greengrocer's first, as supermarkets, again, tend not to stock them as they are difficult to grow without blemishes.

HOW TO PREPARE COOKING APPLES

If you are peeling a large quantity of apples for a large dish, such as apple pie, you will need to stop the apples going brown. Left exposed to the air, apple flesh will go brown in a matter of minutes. The best way to prevent this is to place peeled apples in a bowl of cold water containing lemon juice. If you don't like wasting anything, use the apple peel to make apple tea.

HOW TO BAKE AN APPLE

The only apple to use for baking is, of course, the Bramley. Core the apples and cut the skins all the way round the middle, but no more than skin deep. Place in a buttered baking dish. Combine some rum, brandy or Calvados, sultanas, flaked almonds, mincemeat, brown sugar, cinnamon, grated orange rind and butter in a small mixing bowl, then stuff into the apples. Bake in a preheated oven at gas mark 3/160°C/325°F for 1¼ hours. The apples will fluff up like the best baked potato or soufflé! Serve with double cream.

HOW TO MAKE APPLE SAUCE

Apple sauce isn't just for roast pork. It's wonderful with yoghurt for breakfast, so if it's one of your favourites, treat yourself. Please don't buy one of those ridiculous jars of apple sauce that cost about £1. You only get one or two apples in them, so it is very bad value. Warm 1 tablespoon of butter in a large frying pan, add a few chopped cooking apples, chopped thyme, a bay leaf, nutmeg, cinnamon and about 3 tablespoons of sugar. Add a small glass of water and simmer gently for ½ hour until the apples break down. Taste, and add sugar if necessary. You can mash the sauce if you prefer a smooth apple sauce. Freeze or store in a fridge for up to a week.

PEAR crisp crumble

serves 4-6

8 Conference pears, peeled, cored and sliced

1 dessertspoon grated orange rind

1 tablespoon caster sugar

a pinch of grated nutmeg

6 tablespoons water

25 g/1 oz powdered milk

20 g/¾ oz rolled oats

375 g/12 oz plain flour

200 g/7 oz soft brown sugar

100 g/3½ oz unsalted butter, plus extra for greasing

1 teaspoon ground cinnamon

1 Grease a medium-sized pie dish with some butter. Mix the pears with the orange rind, caster sugar, nutmeg and water and place in the bottom of the dish.

2 Mix the powdered milk, oats, flour, sugar and cinnamon in a large mixing bowl and rub in the butter until crumbly. Smooth the crumble mixture over the pears

3 Bake in a preheated oven at gas mark 6/ 200°C/400°F for about 40 minutes, or until the crumble is brown and crisp and the pear juices starting to bubble to the top. Serve piping hot.

Chocolate-dipped PRUNES

makes 24

24 large prunes, stoned

½ bottle good red wine

4 tablespoons brandy

300 g/10 oz dark chocolate

100 g/3½ oz unsalted butter

1 Soak the prunes in the wine and brandy for at least 8 hours, or for any time up to a month! Just place them in a screw-top jar and keep in a fridge. When you are ready to use, drain well on a wire rack.

2 Line a baking tray with baking parchment. Melt the chocolate and butter

together in a *bain-marie* then remove from the heat.

3 Impale a prune on a skewer then dip into the chocolate, letting any excess drip off. Slip each dipped prune onto the tray. Once you've coated all the prunes, place in a fridge until set.

BREAD &

Bread

Bread has changed beyond recognition. Gone are the days when the only bread available was a white, sliced loaf. If you wanted anything a little different, then you had to rely on a specialist baker, or bake it yourself. But these days, we are spoilt for choice. Most supermarkets have breads from India, Ireland, France, Italy, the USA and Germany to name but a few. Using a variety of ingredients, there is a huge range of textures and taste to choose from. And bread is extremely good for you – healthy, fat-free and filling, we should all eat a lot more of it. Even the humble sandwich needn't be boring – what could be nicer than a large hunk of ciabatta, drizzled with a little extra olive oil, and stuffed with chicken and avocado? Delicious, and packed full of nutrients. I don't propose to tell you how to bake bread – I'd rather give you a few ideas for getting a bit more out of the bread that is available in our supermarkets (and that includes bread soup…).

HOW TO MAKE CROSTINI

Crostini make a very cheap and tasty snack or lunch, or you could serve them to guests with drinks or as a starter. It all depends on what toppings you choose. Take a large French stick, and cut it into 1 cm/⅓ in slices, either into rounds, or into longer, diagonal pieces. I find long slices look more substantial if you are serving crostini as a starter. Heat an oven to gas mark 2/150°C/300°F. Place all your slices on a baking tray and drizzle over some olive oil. Bake until very crispy, which will only be a couple of minutes, so keep an eye on them. Leave to cool, and then rub garlic over the surfaces. Top with whatever you like. Try these if you fancy something very Mediterranean and sunny:

- olive paste (tapenade) with sliced cherry tomatoes
- slice of mozzarella cheese with chopped olives
- red pepper pesto with slices of artichoke
- rocket leaf with a slice of gorgonzola
- smoked fish with sun-dried tomatoes

PASTRY

HOW TO MAKE BRUSCHETTA

This is basically a large version of crostini, but because of the size, the centre of the bread remains soft. Take a small loaf of Italian bread (ciabatta or Bongalesi bread is ideal), and slice lengthways in half. Either bake as we did with the crostini, or grill until lightly toasted. Drizzle with plenty of olive oil.

As you will be eating these with a knife and fork, you can pile up the toppings. These work well:

• rocket leaves, drizzled with olive oil and topped with roasted peppers, anchovies, capers, basil and tomatoes
• a layer of olive paste (tapenade) topped with Parma ham, slices of roast peppers, olives and freshly ground black pepper
• Parma ham, slices of plum tomatoes and mozzarella drizzled with olive oil and seasoned with freshly ground black pepper and grilled until the cheese bubbles. You'll need to assemble this one on a baking sheet before grilling, so it doesn't fall apart.

HOW TO MAKE BREAD SAUCE

This is much easier than you might expect, so I hope you won't bother with a packet mix after reading this. This tastes so much better and it's much more satisfying. As we often serve it with special occasion meals such as Christmas dinner, it's worth making the effort, and you can prepare it in advance. Heat 600 ml/1 pint milk in a pan, with an onion studded with a bay leaf and cloves (use two or three cloves to fasten the bay leaf to the onion). When the milk is simmering, remove the pan from the heat and leave the flavours to infuse for ½ hour. Add about 4 handfuls of fresh breadcrumbs and return to the heat. Cook gently for about 10 minutes until the sauce starts to thicken. Add grated nutmeg, salt and freshly ground black pepper, a knob of butter and a little cream, if you like. If you make this in advance, reheat gently in a *bain-marie*, or in a bowl over a pan of simmering water.

HOW TO MAKE BREADCRUMBS

Why anyone buys breadcrumbs is a complete mystery to me. Do you know any crumbs that go golden yellow? What on earth do they put in the breadcrumbs we can buy? Lots of additives and other strange things probably – and you pay a fortune for them. Simply use stale bread or cheap, sliced bread, crisp it in a low oven, and then whizz it in a food processor.

PANZANELLA

An Italian bread salad –
excellent as a starter.

2 thick slices day-old bread

6 ripe tomatoes, cubed

1 small red onion, finely diced

½ cucumber, diced

1 stick celery, finely sliced

2 cloves garlic, crushed

small handful of fresh basil leaves,
torn into small pieces

4 tablespoons olive oil

1 tablespoon red wine vinegar

salt and freshly ground
black pepper

serves 4

1 Remove the crusts from the bread and cut or tear the bread into small pieces. Place the pieces into a bowl and sprinkle with a little cold water – the bread should be moist but not soggy.

2 Add the tomatoes, onion, cucumber, celery, garlic and basil and mix gently.

3 Mix together the oil and vinegar and season. Shake well to make a dressing and pour over the salad.

4 Toss the salad well, and leave it for 30 minutes before serving to allow the flavours to develop.

Tuscan tomato & BREAD soup

2-3 tablespoons olive oil

1 onion, finely chopped

2 cloves garlic, crushed

1 kg/2 lb ripe tomatoes, peeled, deseeded and chopped

400 g/13 oz tinned, chopped tomatoes

1 small loaf bread, roughly broken

1 bunch basil

serves 6

1 Heat the oil in a large saucepan. Add the onion and garlic. Fry gently until the onion is soft but not brown.

2 Add the fresh tomatoes and cook for 1 minute. Add the tinned tomatoes, bread and basil, reserving a few basil leaves.

3 Simmer for 15 minutes, stirring occasionally. Just before serving, fold in the reserved basil leaves.

White chocolate BREAD & butter pudding

This is guaranteed to go straight to the hips! I like to soak the sultanas beforehand in cold tea, heavily laced with rum – it adds a lovely flavour.

serves 4-6

- 900 ml/1½ pints double cream
- 300 ml/½ pt milk
- 125 g/4 oz caster sugar
- 2 large eggs
- butter, for greasing
- 125 g/4 oz sultanas
- 375 g/12 oz French bread, cut into 1 cm/½ in pieces and lightly toasted
- 150 g/5 oz milk chocolate chips
- 625 g/1¼ lb white chocolate, coarsely chopped

1. Pour the cream and milk into a pan and add the caster sugar. Bring to the boil, and then reduce the heat so the milk is simmering gently. Meanwhile, whisk the eggs until light and frothy.

2. Grease a medium-size baking dish liberally with some butter, and then scatter some of the sultanas around the bottom of the dish. Place a layer of bread on top and then some more sultanas. Scatter a few milk chocolate chips on top.

3. When the sugar has melted in the milk and cream mixture, remove from the heat and add the white chocolate. Stirring constantly, add the whisked eggs. Stir until the chocolate has melted and spoon half of the sauce over the pudding.

4. Add another layer of bread, and some more sultanas and milk chocolate. If you soaked your sultanas in tea and rum, then why not pour in a little of this as well! Cover the dish with the remaining white chocolate sauce and any remaining milk chocolate. Cover with kitchen foil, and leave to stand for about ½ hour.

5. Bake in a preheated oven at gas mark 2/150°C/300°F for 45 minutes. Remove the foil about 5 minutes before the end of the cooking time to colour the top of the pudding.

Pastry

Sorry to disappoint you if you think this bit is going to tell you how to make fabulous pastry. If you really need to know, look on the back of a packet of flour, but I think the pastry products sold in the shops are so good, there really is no need to make your own. You can even buy it in pre-cut rounds now, so it will fit easily into your pie or flan dish. If I have any complaint at all then I'd say that I wish manufacturers would put a little more butter in their pastry, but I'm being very picky. You can use bought shortcrust and puff pastry for all manner of recipes, sweet and savoury. Filo pastry was first invented by the Greeks and you will come across it in delicious Greek and Turkish sweet pastries such as baklava. I was one of the first to use filo pastry in this country at 'Ménage à Trois'.

EASY TOMATO TART

This uses shop-bought puff pastry, and is ridiculously simple. Scatter lots of plain flour over your kitchen surface and roll out a packet of puff pastry to about ½ cm/¼ in and lay it over a well-greased baking tray. Trim away the edges. Spread over a thick layer of passata (bottled tomatoes) leaving a 2 cm/1 in space around the edge, followed by a layer of chopped red onion. Layer over plenty of sliced, ripe tomatoes. Sprinkle with chopped thyme, salt and freshly ground black pepper. Brush the edge with egg yolk, and drizzle olive oil over the tomatoes. Bake in a preheated oven at gas mark 6/200°C/400°F for 15-18 minutes, or until the pastry is golden brown.

HOW TO 'BLIND BAKE' PASTRY

This is a very useful technique, because once you have mastered making a pastry case, you can fill it with all manner of delicious things. Scatter lots of plain flour over your kitchen surface and roll out a packet of shortcrust pastry. Lift it over a well-greased quiche mould and push it into the corners. Roll a rolling pin over the top, to trim off the excess pastry. If you have any holes, simply fill using pieces of leftover pastry. Prick the pastry all over using a fork, and put in a fridge for ½ hour to rest. Line with greaseproof paper, fill with dried beans and bake in a preheated oven at gas mark 4/180°C/350°F for 10-15 minutes. When the pastry is set, remove the paper and beans and bake for a further 5 minutes or until light brown.

EASY QUICHE

This is a great way to use a blind-baked pastry case. It's more creamy quiche than the rubbery type you might be familiar with. Melt a knob of butter in a large frying pan and fry 2-3 sliced courgettes. When

just brown, reserve to one side. Add 4-5 sliced leeks and cook until softened, then add 125 g/4 oz of crumbled Gorgonzola cheese, plenty of grated Parmesan, some torn parsley, rocket and oregano. Mix well, and pour into the pastry case. Beat together a splash of cream, 3 eggs and 1 egg yolk, whisk until light and frothy, then pour into the pastry case. Using a fork, gently mix so the liquid covers the vegetables. Arrange the cooled courgettes over the surface, and bake the quiche in a preheated oven at gas mark 4/180°C/350°F for 25-30 minutes. To test the quiche, insert a knife, and if it comes out clean, the quiche is cooked.

CHICKEN KORMA PIE

This is a very easy way to use filo pastry. It looks and tastes great, so it's a good way to impress your friends. Brush the sheets of filo pastry with melted butter, and layer them in a buttered quiche dish, butter-side down. Make sure you have plenty of overlap – you will probably need to use at least 8 sheets. Make holes in the bottom with a fork, and then tip in 2 small packets or tins of ready-made chicken korma. Season well, and add plenty of chopped coriander. Starting with the last sheet of pastry, bring the edge into the centre of the chicken with a twist. Continue with all the sheets until you have closed the pie with a decorative pile of pastry. If your pastry doesn't quite meet, then scrunch up a couple more sheets of pastry, and tuck into the centre of the pie. Bake in a preheated oven at gas mark 4/180°C/350°F for 20-25 minutes or until the pastry turns golden brown.

RECIPE INDEX